THE

MASTERS BOOK OF
SNOOK

SECRETS OF TOP SKIPPERS

by Frank Sargeant

Book 2 in the Saltwater Series

Larsen's Outdoor Publishing

ISBN 0-936513-48-9

Library of Congress 97-070713

Published by:

LARSEN'S OUTDOOR PUBLISHING
2640 Elizabeth Place
Lakeland, FL 33813
FAX 941/644-3288

PRINTED IN THE UNITED STATES OF AMERICA

1 2 3 4 5 6 7 8 9 10

2

ACKNOWLEDGEMENTS

Ron Taylor, Jim Whittington, Mike Tringali and Ed Irby of Florida's Department of Environmental Protection have all been helpful in providing research information on snook, much of it never before published in the popular press. Dr. Craig Whitehead, who has probably caught more of the 12 species of snook than any other angler alive, also shared his knowledge. Randy Edwards and Carole Neidig of Mote Marine were also generous. And the work of Dr. Luis Rivas of the University of Miami Marine Science Department was the basis for the chapter on distribution of snook species.

Captains Eric Bachnik, Mark Bennett, Jim Bradley, Lee Edrington, Pete Greenan, John Griffith, Paul Hawkins, Van Hubbard, David Fairbanks, Dave Justice, Richard Knox, Ky Lewis, Steve Love, Dave Markett, Steve Marusak, Rob McCue, Larry Mendez, Bill Miller, Chris Mitchell, Scott Moore, Brian Mowatt, Mark Nichols, Dave Pomerleau, Dennis Royston, Doc Selig, Richard Seward, Mike Talkington, Ray Van Horn, Johnnie Walker, Jerry Williams and James Wisner — master snookers all — shared their knowledge with me.

Particular credit goes to Captain Russ Sirmons, who not only taught me a lot about snook, but also carved the superb glass sculpture decorating the cover. Sirmons' one-of-a-kind works are now collectors' items throughout the South. He can be reached at (813) 526-2090 in St. Petersburg, Florida.

Finally, thanks to Bill LeMaster and the folks at L & S Baits, who were kind enough to sponsor this book. The LeMasters have made MirrOlures the world's most popular snook lures for generations, as well as backing endless conservation efforts that have made it possible for snook and snook country to survive Florida's explosive growth.

ABOUT THE AUTHOR

Former flats guide Frank Sargeant is one of America's best-known outdoors writers. His work has won more than 50 national awards and has appeared in most major magazines in the outdoors and boating fields.

He is author of nine other fishing titles including the best-selling SNOOK BOOK, the Inshore Series and the Coastal Fishing Guides (Secret Spots Series). He is a world-renowned expert in flats fishing. Sargeant is a former editor for CBS Publishing Division and senior writer for Walt Disney World Marketing. He has been outdoors editor of the Tampa Tribune for more than 12 years and is a masthead editor for a number of outdoors magazines. He's former president of the Florida Outdoor Writers Association. He holds a masters in English from Ohio University and has taught writing at the high school and college levels.

Sargeant has fished for snook for over 30 years throughout Florida and Central America with many of the world's best snook skippers and anglers. He lives on the Little Manatee River in Ruskin, Florida.

CONTENTS

INTRODUCTION
THE ZEN OF SNOOKING

It's a largemouth bass on steroids.

It's the Enterprise at Warp 11.

It's faster than a speeding bullet, more powerful than a locomotive, able to leap tall mangroves at a single bound.

It's the uncommon common snook.

The snook, *Centropomis undecimalis,* has the unique ability to accelerate in all three dimensions at once when it feels the hook. It even transmigrates into a fourth dimension at times, dematerializing in open water, reappearing deep inside a mangrove tangle with your prize plug hanging from its jaw like a stubby Ybor City cigar.

It is, for thousands of saltwater anglers, the ultimate fish.

A snook slams a surface bait like no other finny creature. Picture a weight-lifter in a 'roid rage. AAARRRRGGGGHHH!! Linesiders bend hooks, bust rods and snap lures in half, all in a microsecond. And the fish that come exploding through the surface may weigh as much as 40 pounds.

It's not fishing for the weak of heart.

This is a book dedicated to those who already know and love snook, and who understand the basics. If you're still on square one, you might take a look at my first effort in the field, The Snook Book, which is still available in many tackle shops and bookstores around Florida or direct from my pal and publisher, Larry Larsen (see the Resource Directory on page 151). That one covers basic tackle, tactics and snook habitat.

This book, on the other hand, presumes that you know a 52-M from a 7-M, how to tie a Uni-Knot and a Bimini and generally understand the seasonal migrations of the fish. It's a book dedicated

Snook are big, powerful and fast, and they're found in some of the most beautiful estuaries on the globe. For many anglers, they're the ultimate gamefish. (MirrOlure photo)

to fine-tuning your skills, and more particularly to catching really big snook, the ones that are so elusive for most of us.

This is a book about where snook go when they become hard to find, and how to make them bite when they've got lockjaw. It contains the tips and tricks I've learned from a lifetime of pursuing the ultimate gamefish, and even more importantly the combined knowledge of dozens of the world's finest snook anglers who have been generous enough to share their boats with me.

It also contains more biological information on snook than has ever before been published in the popular press, including details on the 12 recognized species of the Atlantic and Pacific, as well as the latest on genetic variations in common snook in their U.S. range.

It's a book for the enthusiast, the guy who has snook plates on his car and a line of expired snook tags taped to his office wall. It's a book for snookaholics, for addicts whose only fix is getting a line on a linesider. In short, it's a book for snook masters.

A WORD OF CAUTION
(A FEW WORDS FROM FRANK'S LAWYER)

Fishing in snook country, particularly after sundown, can be dangerous business. Nothing in this book should be construed as encouraging the inexperienced boatman to reach beyond his abilities, or to omit the precautions required by common sense.

Fishing safely requires a seaworthy boat, properly maintained. It requires experience in handling a boat in all sea conditions. It requires a full complement of safety gear and marine electronics. And operating in the shallows calls for a constant eye on depth.

Backup systems are also highly recommended for radio communications and navigation—and for battery power, without which neither of these electronic systems have any use. And no wise skipper ever leaves the docks without checking the weather report—and his bilge pumps.

The major worry in fishing after dark is running your boat into an unlighted obstruction—most commonly a navigation marker put there to keep you safe! The cement pilings of these markers don't give. I know a guy in Stuart who put a three-foot divot in the bow of his rig one night, and launched himself in a cannon shot over the bow. He wasn't hurt, but don't bet that you'll be so lucky. Slow and careful is the rule after sundown, and keep the spotlight at your side.

Snook themselves have the potential to do some damage to anglers. Their gill covers are knife-edged and can inflict painful cuts. And the multiple-hook plugs and live bait rigs can also be dangerous—especially when they come loose under pressure as the fish nears the boat. A flopping snook can also manage to bury any loose hooks into your fingers, hands or feet.

Those without the appropriate gear and knowledge should approach live fish with extreme care. In short, there are a number of ways you can get hurt pursuing this sport. Overall, you're a lot safer out reeling in snook than driving in highway traffic around any urban area these days. But it's always wise to be prepared and be cautious.

CHAPTER 1

FISH OF DREAMS
MASTERING TROPHY SNOOK

Really big snook, the fish of dreams, are as different from the little guys as they are from redfish or trout. Learning to catch the giants—over a yard long—is a tough game, but one that most expert snookers eventually turn to when simply catching any snook is no longer a challenge. (Hah—it should ever get that easy!)

BIOLOGY OF GIANT SNOOK

Biologists have discovered that nearly all snook over 20 inches long are female—they believe the males reverse sex as they age. It takes a snook about three to four years to reach the minimum legal size on Florida's east coast, and about four to five years to reach that size on the west coast. It takes an added four to eight years for a 24-inch legal fish to reach the 40-inch length that identifies a real trophy for most experienced snookers.

West coast female snook grow two to four inches per year after reaching the minimum two-foot legal size, east coast fish a bit faster. On either coast, warm weather and plenty of bait produces maximum growth, while cold winters and poor feed caused by pollution or red tide can cut the growth in half. Total age for a 40-incher is likely to be between 8 and 16 years.

LENGTH AND WEIGHT

Incidentally, a 40-incher is not nearly as heavy, usually, as it looks. Usually, a west coast fish of that length will go around 22 to 28 pounds, an east coaster several pounds more. (They LOOK like

I didn't know they got that big, Captain Dave Pomerleau seems to be saying. This monster fish may be the unoffical state record, but it was not entered under IGFA rules.

30 pounds, don't they?) However, every added inch on a fish this size can add 2 to 3 1/2 pounds, depending on condition.

Florida's unofficial state record, caught by Dave Pomerleau in 1995, was 49 inches long and went 44 pounds 11 ounces. The 53-pound, 10-ounce all-tackle record from Costa Rica was 54 inches long—about a pound per inch! Note, though, that snook don't follow the formula that works so well for tarpon, length X girth squared divided by 800. Pomerleau's fish had a girth of 29.5 inches, and based on that it should have weighed 53.3 pounds via the formula.

A fish caught illegally January 15, 1989 in the Hillsborough River in Tampa was reportedly 50 inches long, had a girth of 30 inches and a weight of 45 pounds, 15 ounces according to the guy who poached it. It should have weighed 56.25 pounds via the formula. So, a better estimate for snook 40 inches and up is:

Length x girth squared divided by 900.

This won't be exact, but it's a lot closer than using an 800 divisor, and gives you a ballpark figure for trophy fish you release without weighing.

It should be noted that biologists report not many snook survive beyond their eighth year on the west coast during normal weather fluctuations. However, on the east coast, where the fish average considerably larger due to warmer water and perhaps to the slight genetic variation, many reach 10 to 12 years, and the oldest fish ever aged was 21. (Oddly enough, Dave Pomerleau's 44 pound, 11 ounce monster was aged at the DEP labs in St. Petersburg and found to be only 11 years old—the Shaq O'Neill of snook!)

THE HUNT FOR LUNKERS

Why don't anglers catch more really big snook?

First, there are not that many of them. Angling pressure, killing cold and predators prevent most fish from living long enough to become lunkers. (Porpoises home in on snook above all other flats species except maybe mullet.)

So you're seeking those fish that managed to escape the actuarial tables when you go after the 40-inch-plus monster. Resign yourself. You're not going to catch a fish this size every day, or even every month.

Professional guides on the water close to 300 days a year land only a few of this size annually. Of course, part of the reason is that there are few guides who target big fish and only big fish. Clients usually want action rather than a long wait between bites, so the pros tailor their trips for lots of small to medium fish rather than going for the single home run.

LAND OF THE GIANTS

The second reason catches of lunker snook are rare is that most live in or near deep water—they rarely venture on the flats or into the mangroves where most snook anglers fish. Gulf and Atlantic passes, piers along the outer beaches, seawalled canals, deep-water bridges and shipping harbors are the primary habitat of the giants. Since maybe 90 percent of the fishing pressure for snook is on the flats and in mangrove creeks and bays, the anglers are not fishing where the big gals live.

Big snook may have been flats dwellers historically, but these days the combination of harvest pressure and boat traffic appears to have moved most to deeper water. Their only visits to the shallows are likely to come after dark when both fishermen and boaters are off the water.

In that way, they're somewhat like trophy whitetail deer— while you may see dozens of young bucks in open meadows early and late in the day, the only time that 10-pointer shows is after dark. Otherwise, he's in the heaviest cover where hunters can't get at him. Lunker snook are similarly cautious.

The big fish are probably most abundant near the passes, ICW bridges and coastal piers. They're not disturbed there by the passage of boats because of the depth, they're not visible to anglers, and the superior water quality in these areas keeps food always available.

But they also love the 40- to 50-foot depths of ship basins and commercial wharves, areas where tangles of junk on the bottom provide them lots of cover, and where anglers rarely venture. The water quality in these areas may leave something to be desired, but there are always plenty of mullet and young snapper around as food. And the water temperatures remain comfortable year-around, so these giants rarely have reason to leave.

16

Lunkers like this one are sometimes caught on small sardines, but a better plan for trophies is to use larger baits like mojarra, mullet or ladyfish. Large deep-diver plugs can also catch plenty of big snook.

THEY CAN HANDLE A WHOPPER

Elephants may eat peanuts, but they more often eat hay bales. And big snook usually prefer baits a lot larger than the typical angler fishes. Live ladyfish a foot long, half-pound mullet or grunts and 6-inch thread herring or greenbacks are more likely to attract the attention of a giant than the typical 4-inch sardine or 1/4 ounce jig. Among plugs, jumbos divers like the 107 or 113 MirrOlure trolled deep in the passes are the tickets.

Using the specialized live baits requires a fishing trip before you go fishing; you may have to put in several hours casting for ladyfish or jigging up big greenies, and you'll need a jumbo live well to keep a half-dozen baits alive.

One note on using ladyfish and mullet—they're such a big mouthful that most snook can't inhale them in one gulp. You may see an awful lot of thrashing around before the fish actually has the bait, but don't be in a hurry to set the hook. If the fish is a true trophy, it can readily swallow even the largest bait, but these lunkers are in no hurry. They're not like school fish rushing to eat a sardine before their brothers can grab it.

Remember, too, that most predators tend to grab a large prey by the head and swallow it that way, so put your hook in the nose rather than in the back. (Of course, for fish that you're going to release, you don't want to let them have the bait too long—hopefully, you set while the hook is still in the mouth rather than down in the throat or stomach.)

There are times, though, when a dorsal hook placement is the only choice. If you need to steer a bait into a tangle of low pilings or under overhanging mangroves, you can manage that a lot better by light tugs on a hook placed just behind the dorsal fin than with one through the nose or mouth. It's possible to direct a bait to swim many yards into cover where you could never place a cast, and often these are the very spots where the biggest snook hide. Of course, getting them out is another matter!

There's a temptation to use stinger hooks, trebles dangling on a bit of heavy leader near the tail, with big baits. They definitely increase the number of hookups. But stingers are often a death sentence for the fish they catch.

If a treble goes deep into a fish's throat, she probably won't survive. Do you really want to go out with gear that's going to kill every trophy you catch?

Using big jigs and plugs is less risky for the fish. And a jumbo diving plug trolled deep around the edges of pass dropoffs, bridge pilings and shipping docks is an excellent way to connect with a giant. Trolling big lures also allows you to cover a lot of water rapidly, a big help when you're learning the haunts of the lunkers.

SCAVENGER-HUNT

Big fish are also more prone to scavenging than younger, more active snook. One of the favorite techniques of Captain James Wisner of Tampa is to fish a whole dead shad, about 10 inches long, on the bottom in areas like Port Tampa and Port Manatee after dark.

You catch plenty of sailcats and sharks with this tactic, but you also catch snook measured by the yard.

Lunkers sometimes prowl wadefishing territory, but most often they're caught on the outer edges of the flats, in outer passes or around shipping channels and basins. (MirrOlure photo)

TACKLING THE JUMBOS

It usually takes some very serious tackle to land these lunkers—as the saying goes, you don't go bear hunting with a switch. In areas where there are lots of pilings or sunken trash, many lunker-hunters go to 100-pound-test mono, 7/0 forged hooks, 4/0 reels and rods designed to whip 6-foot tarpon—and they still get broken off regularly!

Captain Jerry Williams of Tampa, who has dredged his share of monsters from around the shipyards downtown, suggests nylon-coated cable rather than even the heaviest mono as insurance against being cut off on the pilings when you fish live bait. However, Williams gets more than his share by some deft work with a stout baitcaster, a 7m and 20-pound-test mono.

Of course, when you pursue large fish in the passes, much lighter gear can be used, particularly if you fish from a boat. Twenty-pound tackle is plenty, and it's possible to beat the big ones on 8 if you're good and patient. However, remember that the longer you fight the fish, the less chance it has to survive release and to avoid sharks and porpoises after being released—try to keep your fighting time under 10 minutes by choosing tackle that suits the task.

Where do you find the giants? There are a number of spots around the southern half of the state noted for producing trophies.

LAND O' LUNKERS

In Tampa Bay there are enormous, dredged basins throughout the downtown area of Tampa where the shipbuilders and steel dealers ply their trade, with 30- to 50-foot deep cuts extending to the mouth of the Hillsborough River near Harbor Island and all the way to the outflow from McKay Bay near the 22nd Street Causeway. There are numerous docks over the water here, and some lunker-hunters use small jon boats to prowl back among the pilings, delivering big baits to fish that would never see a hook and line otherwise.

The Port Sutton Powerplant, also downtown, provides a steady flow of bath-warm water into a 30-foot deep channel year around, and particularly in winter, big snook use this area as a temperature refuge. A fair number also cruise into the Hillsborough River in winter.

Move south to the Alafia River and the big docks of the phosphate company near the river mouth also provide deep water and lots of tangled cover where big fish thrive. There's also a warm-water outflow here—it's smaller than that of the electric companies, but enough to provide a refuge for the fish, and the Alafia has numerous springs upriver that keep it warmer than the bay in winter.

Big snook love a big mouthful like this grunt. Jumbo baits tend to separate the dinks from the dinosaurs, though sometimes it's a long time between bites.

Big Bend Powerplant is a few miles south of the Alafia. It has a hot water outflow on the south side that always holds big winter snook, though the prime fishing area is now blocked off as a manatee spa. And the deeper barge basins on the north side hold some large fish, as well.

South of Ruskin is Port Manatee and its adjoining spoil island, both noted spots for big snook. The whoppers move to the west tip of the island to spawn in summer, but as October turns to November, they head for the deeper waters inside the port.

Port Tampa, just south of Gandy Causeway on the Tampa side, is another noted spot for monster snook, and several Bay area fishermen claim to have tangled with 50-pounders there. Fish of around 40 pounds have been landed.

On the west side of the Gandy is the Weedon Island Powerplant, with a warm water outflow on the north side. This is a shallow cut, but it's good on winter mornings before it's disturbed by boat traffic. There's a deep barge basin on the east, good all year, and probably superior for really big fish because of the pods of foot-long mullet it attracts.

Finally, there's the Skyway itself—one of the few prime snook areas that can be reached by anglers without boats. The massive bait flow and the endless exchange of deep, clean water through the bridge pilings makes this great habitat for big fish. The rockpiles around the pylons are excellent if you have a boat, but plenty of big fish are hooked directly from the fishing pier spans, too. The small bridge on the south side has 14 feet of water flowing under it, and is a great after-dark spot for lunkers.

Big snook also hang around the pilotboat docks on the back side of Egmont Key, where they're just a swish of the tail from endless baitfish and very deep water.

CHARLOTTE HARBOR

Another prime area for giants is Charlotte Harbor, a southern copy of Tampa Bay, but with more seagrass and better water quality. The old phosphate docks at Boca Grande Pass have produced tons of fish over 20 pounds for decades. So have the lower Peace and Myakka rivers, which hold lunkers from about November through March.

Don't overlook the smaller passes in this area—San Carlos, Redfish, Captiva and Little Gasparilla and Stump are all superior spots to go lunker-hunting. So are docks along deeper portions of the Intracoastal Waterway throughout these waters from Sarasota southward to Marco.

THE EVERGLADES

The big rivers of the 10,000 Islands and the Everglades have always been lunker country. They're not as remote as they once were, but they still get less pressure than waters farther north and also have fewer cold-kills, so they produce lots of very large fish.

The big, deep rivers are better than the smaller creeks when you look for trophies. Check out Lostman, Rodgers, Broad, Harney, Shark, Little Shark and Joe rivers, paying particular attention to points where side creeks join the main flow and to undercut banks. For details, see the chapter on fishing the Everglades.

EAST COAST

The submarine basin at Canaveral is becoming famed for producing monsters from its 60-foot depths. Because the water is so deep, it provides year-around refuge, and the closed areas inside the military base offer a hideaway that acts as a reservoir for big mamas cruising into the open waters after dark.

Fort Pierce, Port St. Lucy and Palm Beach inlets are noted for 40-pound fish, as are many of the passes, bridges and canals from Lauderdale south through Miami Beach. See the chapter on East Coast waters for details. Also, at the back of this book, you can check out the "Secret Spots" series for detailed where-to-fish information and marked NOAA charts.

CLOSE BUT NO CIGAR

Speaking of giant fish, Florida has flirted with the all-tackle record several times in recent years. A few winters back a 60-inch plus fish was reported caught and released in Sarasota Pass during the closed season, and a fish of 61.5 inches was caught and released by Don King of Nocatee, fishing a live ladyfish on a Calcutta pole at a bridge on Pine Island Sound in 1994.

Neither of these fish were photographed, but both were caught by big-snook specialists noted for their ability to produce giants. If the fishermen didn't stretch the truth, their fish were certainly world-class—very probably close to 60 pounds!

The all-tackle world record fish, 4'6" long, was taken in Costa Rica, where the fish tend to be short and fat for their weight. Even considering that our fish here are more lanky, a five-footer would have to be awfully close to the world mark.

(Dave Pomerleau's apparent Florida state record fish was not entered with the IGFA. Pomerleau did not weigh the fish in until some 24 hours after he reportedly caught it, and did not submit it for Torry-meter testing to check for time of death. This lead a number of anglers to protest the circumstances of the catch. Rather than hold a shadowed record, Pomerleau says he's going to catch another one even bigger.)

LIVE AND LET LIVE

For those who do luck into a giant, it's well to remember that these fish are 10 to 15 years old and will take a long time to replace if you kill them. The meat of these lunkers is coarse and sometimes less than tasty, and perhaps not all that safe considering how long some live in the polluted environment of the harbors. A photograph will provide the memories, and if you want a mount, simply take the length and girth measurements and pass them along to the taxidermist—all snook mounts are done in fiberglass these days, so the carcass is not needed. Better to let that giant go back and put on a few more pounds, to provide an even greater challenge the next time you visit.

CHAPTER 2

MASTERING THE TIDES

Show me a master snook angler and I'll show you a guy who reads the tide tables before breakfast and maybe again after dinner. He may forget his wedding anniversary, but he won't forget the date of the spring tides in May. (This may have something to do with the high divorce rate among snook fishermen.)

No fish are more reactive to tidal flow than snook. They depend on the flowing water to bring food to them almost like rainbow trout in a mountain stream. When the water isn't moving, they rarely feed.

But there's a lot to learn besides what time of day high and low tides come in your fishing area. You know the basics: tides are very long, low ocean waves caused by the pull of the moon and the sun. They're not evident at sea, but when they hit land the motion of the waves causes the water to rise and fall, and also creates tidal currents as the water flows over shallows and through narrow passages. Anyone who spends any time around the coast knows this much. But the flow varies dramatically based on the shape of the land it meets.

PLAYING THE TIDES

Tide heights are listed in distances above or below the mean low tide at a given spot — the "zero" line. The greater the variations from zero — that is, the taller the wave — the stronger the tide flow and usually the better the fishing.

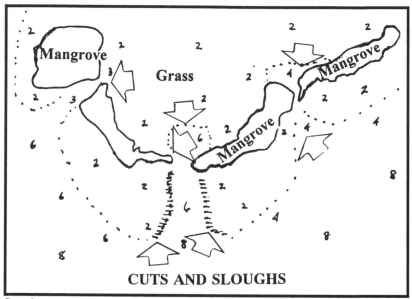

CUTS AND SLOUGHS

Snook restaurants are usually in areas where they can take advantage of "choke points" in the terrain. On incoming flows, the outer bars are the first spot to try, followed by the island points. On the outflow, the points are again good early, followed by the deeper channels as the water drops.

However, you have to take what the tides give you, and a great snooker plays the ebb and flow like a master violinist working through a symphony. (Or maybe more like a banjo picker working through "Dueling Banjos".)

Tides follow wider, deeper channels first. In a bayou fed by several tidal creeks you may see that the inflow begins on the main arm and is already flowing strong there while it's dead or even going out on the smaller feeders.

Time your fishing to take advantage of this, hitting the big feeder first, then the smaller ones as they "wake up" and begin to flow. The best fishing in all these small passes, incidentally, is usually on the downtide side of the points, that is on the inside on incoming water and the outside on outgoing water. These spots create eddies that allow the snook to avoid the flow, yet easily pick off baits swirled in. And if there happens to be a pothole curving around the

26

point, as there often is due to current scouring, you've discovered a super snook spot.

The tide comes into an estuary in a plume that you can see on the surface when the water is calm. It has a rounded leading edge, and it stays discrete for a time from the residual water left in the backcountry on the previous low—differences in salinity or temperature probably account for the edge. Baitfish often ride this plume, and as it passes a feeding station snook begin to strike.

THE PULSE OF THE ESTUARIES

Tides flow in cycles or pulses within their larger movements. Particularly on the rise there may be an hour of strong flow, then a lull of 30 minutes to an hour, then another several hours of strong flow all within a given incoming tide. These are the reverse flows that swell to become full outgoing tides on four-tide days, but in the interim they're simply hesitations in the incoming flow.

Falls tend to be more straight ahead, which is why they are stronger and often produce the best action of the day, but they also have occasional "periods" when they slow down.

The fish usually respond to these minor changes; you may have hot fishing on the start of the rise, then a dead time, then another major feed. And when all the water dumps out at once, going from say a plus 2.9 to a minus 0.40, over three feet of water has to get out of the back country in a period of 6 to 8 hours.

This means strong flows for a long period of time, and that means you'll have lots of opportunities to throw to fish that are in a feeding mode. (Note that "strong" flows in snook country are not anything like strong flows farther north along the Atlantic Coast, where tide ranges of 8 feet are common. We're talking relative flows here, not absolutes.)

SPRING TIDES

Around the new and full moon periods there is one major high and one major low daily, and the magnitude is much greater than at other times of the month. These are known as "spring" tides, even though they occur in every month.

Between the major tides on these phases is a minor rise followed by a very brief fall. For example, on December 24, 1996 at St. Pete Pier, the high tide was +2.20 at 12:47 a.m. There was a major, continuous fall to -0.50 by 8:40 a.m. The minor incoming tide then rose to +1.26 by 3:50 p.m., fell slightly to +1.03 by 7:27 p.m., and then continued its rise back to +2.16 by 1.23 a.m. at which point it was ready for another major fall. Pay attention to these changes — they can become part of your fishing pattern.

NEAP TIDES

Compare this to the half-moon periods and you see that there are two nearly equal highs and two lows each 24 hours during these times. Less water is moving on each tide, but about every six hours you have a significant flow. These are called "neap" tides.

It makes sense to try to fish the major fall on spring tides around the new and full moons because this is when the water is moving fastest and the fish are most likely to be active. In the intermediate or neap tide periods, all tides are pretty much equal so the choice is up to you. Remember that the tides repeat themselves on two-week cycles, so if you had good fishing on a morning rise at a given spot, go back there 14 days later and you'll probably have the same sort of action unless there's a major weather change in the mean time.

And the tides also pretty much repeat themselves each year on a given moon cycle, so if there's a 2.90 high tide on this year's December full moon, it will be about the same next December. (Remember that the full moon won't come on the same date, though, if you're planning a trip far in advance.)

TIDE SENSE

Watch natural tidal indicators to get a feel for the movement— the way a stick or a buoy carves the surface can tell you volumes about where and how you ought to be fishing. Take what the water gives you—many days, you'll find that the published tide tables and God don't agree.

My advice: listen to God.

Fish the fast water, where ever and when ever you find it, and don't worry if it doesn't agree with the tables. It's learning to read the real-time clues, these small parts of the grand puzzle, that make snook fishing so challenging and so interesting.

In general, current speeds are controlled by the difference between the highs and lows, and the time from the high to the low— lots of water moving over a short period of time means strong

High water usually means it's time to fish docks and mangrove shorelines. Some spots may produce only a few days each month when tides are ideal.

currents and probably good fishing if you're in the right spots at the right time. However, it also pays to understand how the geography of an estuary affects current speeds. Anywhere that lots of water has to fit through a narrow gap between islands or bars there will be a strong flow.

Some of these areas are very obvious, as in the main slough coming out of a large bayou—the entrance channels to Turtle Bay and Bull Bay at Charlotte Harbor and Bishop's Harbor and Cockroach Bay at Tampa Bay are classic examples.

In fact, the currents in those areas have created the channels, which are 6 to 8 feet deep, but surrounded by flats that are only 1 to 3 feet deep. Seek out similar spots on a chart when you plan to visit a new area for the first time, and chances are you'll find good fishing.

Points along a shoreline can also cause increased tidal speeds as the water stacks up and hurries around the obstruction. These areas are tiny, but they can be very good.

Big snook are more inclined to feed on strong tide flows. Mature snook seek out the prime feeding stations where the parade of food is most generous. (MirrOlure photo)

SNOOK RESTAURANTS

OK, so you know the general highway where you're likely to find fish, but where are the restaurants on that highway? These are the feeding stations within the current areas that consistently attract snook. The obvious ones are the oyster bars, channel edges, docks, bridge abutments, jetties and mangrove points.

Less obvious but sometimes even more productive are underwater rock piles like those in the Fakka Union River just beyond the Port of The Islands Channel. Spots like this are gold because the average shoreline fisherman never sees them, so fish there are not often molested. You find them by watching your depthfinder for abrupt outcroppings in the bottom, or by watching the surface for upwellings during strong tide flows, a sign that an obstruction below is altering the flow.

The edges of potholes on high-energy grass flats like those scattered throughout the Indian River, Pine Island Sound and lower

Tampa Bay are also snook diners. The difference between a good pothole and a poor one is usually tide flow—lots of flow, lots of snook; not much flow, not many snook. Always keep your eyes open for a hole anywhere you notice the current is in a big hurry.

Snook prefer to attack bait that is not out in open water. There are times when you'll luck into a school of linesiders that are out in the middle of a big Everglades river or at the mouth of an east coast inlet blasting mullet up into the air, but much more often they're likely to be around some sort of cover waiting for the bait to come by close enough for a surprise attack.

Snook have the speed to run down baits, but it's more their nature to make a quick, sudden attack from cover like a lion than to run down their prey in the open like a cheetah. Find an area where tide moves bait over cover and you've got a snook hideout.

SEASONAL VARIATIONS

Summer tides are generous, winter tides are stingy. Remember that when you think about running your boat across a shallow flat on a December full-moon low. In summer, the only tides that go below mean low or zero are the spring tides on the few days around the new and full moon. But in winter, it's not uncommon for a week on either side of the moons to be at or below zero at extreme low.

For example, on the full moon in May of 1996, the lowest tide was -0.27 at St. Petersburg Pier in Tampa Bay. On the December full moon at the same spot, the lowest tide was -0.50, about three inches lower. That doesn't sound like a lot, but it's enough to make thousands of acres go bare in the gentle topography of Florida's west coast. It's also enough to ruin your lower unit.

The highs are higher in spring and summer, as well—the max on the June, 1996 full moon was +2.91 at St. Pete, while the high on the December full was just +2.20, more than .7 foot lower. Why is it this way? I could tell you, but then I'd have to kill all the real tidal experts who would call up and tell me that I didn't get it exactly right. It happens — that's all we really need to know.

WIND TIDES

The predicted tides are based on the pull of the moon, sun and Earth, but they can't take into account the effect of winds. In winter on Florida's west coast, it's very common to get 20- to 30- knot winds out of the northeast after a front, and these can move another 6 inches to a foot of water out on the extreme lows. Conversely, these same winds pile water into the inlets on the east coast.

And in summer, strong winds out of the southwest are not uncommon. These tend to make the already tall summer tides even higher. On the east coast, the Trade Winds that blow from the east over southern Florida make their high tides taller in summer.

What does this tell us as anglers? First, that even if temperatures remain moderate in winter, the fish might well change locations. Extreme lows may mean that fish normally living on a flat will have to fall into a pothole, swash channel or creek where they never go in summer. In summer, extreme highs may move fish well back into mangroves or up on flats that are otherwise too shallow for them to prowl, and these are good areas to prospect when fish become hard to find elsewhere.

TIDE TABLES

As a newspaper writer, I frequently get calls from people wanting to know why the tides in their fishing spot don't seem to match those published in the paper. The usual reason for this (omitting my occasional incompetent transfer of information) is that they are fishing somewhere that's actually several miles from the station for which the tide has been calculated.

The time of high tide at St. Petersburg Pier might be an hour or more different from the time for the high at the head of Riviera Bay, just a few miles inside Tampa Bay. That's because the water has to work its way through a number of narrow passages and across shallow flats to get there. These slow the wave and retard the times of the highs and lows.

In fact, knowing this, you can learn to follow the tide, fishing the maximum flow at a number of locations as it works its way in from the gulf or ocean and then back out. It's the mark of a master snooker to stay on the peak of the tide, working it all day long as prime time comes and goes at dozens of spots. (For those with computers, TideMaster tide charts are super for planning your trips on prime tides as much as a year into the future. For details, contact Zephyr Services, 1900 Murray Avenue, Pittsburgh, PA 15217.)

CHAPTER 3

TACTICS OF SNOOK MASTERS

You can catch plenty of fish by fishing only after sundown and using only live bait. Hey, that's the easy way. We don't want that, do we? For those fishermen who can't shuffle their work and family hours to fit the schedule of the midnight ramblers, or who just plain don't like casting livies into the black hole, careful attention to tactics can bear fruit after the sun rises.

FIND ACTIVE FISH

Snook are notorious for feeding during very short periods each day. When they decide to eat, the food frenzy may be intense, but it may be over in 10 minutes, too. Then the fish eat little or nothing until the next cycle, perhaps 24 hours later, perhaps even longer.

Further, they're very sensitive to fishing pressure. When a school first settles into an area during the seasonal movements, they're likely to be quick to hit anything appetizing that comes near on a strong tide flow, but after they've had a few lures buzz over their heads, the whole school gets finicky.

There are two possible approaches to the problems. One is the "run-and-gun", which is to fish a lot of different spots, moving every 30 minutes until you find an area where there are lots of fish that haven't been disturbed and which are in a feeding mood. This takes an investment of energy and fuel, but if you do it regularly you build up a catalog of areas likely to produce. This is the way to go if you prefer artificials and if you get fidgety sitting in one spot.

THE RIGHT BAIT

The other tack is what might be called the Scott Moore approach, which is to work known schools of fish, but to make them an offer they can't refuse—that is to present them with their favorite food in large quantities, creating what rainbow trout fishermen would call a "hatch"—and forcing a feeding period to begin.

Moore, Larry Mendez, Van Hubbard and others who practice the art, toss handfuls of live scaled sardines out over holes in the flats, around groins along the beach, in swash channels on falling water, and in the passes during the May-July spawn. If there are snook present, they often respond to the sudden abundance of their favorite food by turning on to a quick feed, even though their natural feeding cycle might be hours away.

Once the fish start exploding on the "free" food, a sardine with a light hook and no weight is put into the same area. The results are usually immediate and violent.

For those who can't handle a castnet or don't want to invest several hours in finding bait before each day of fishing, live shrimp work almost as well as sardines when fished the same way—using plenty to chum a hole, then fishing them free-lined.

LIGHTER TACKLE?

In clear water, lighter tackle is often the difference between success and failure. While a linesider up a murky Everglades creek will readily bust a noisy topwater fished on 25-pound test with a 40-pound-test leader, the fish will pay no attention to an offering on such hawser in the winter-clear waters of St. Lucie Inlet or Pine Island Sound.

Some very knowledgeable anglers are switching to spinning tackle and 8-pound-test mono for this reason when fishing the clearer flats. With a leader of 20-pound-test clear or pale green mono, the thinner stuff draws far more hits.

The problem in fishing spinning gear is that the typical rods tend to be as wimpy as the line, and that's not effective for working topwater lures, nor for controlling heavy fish. The best spinning rod for sizable topwaters is very stiff, with about the whip of a fencing rapier, though it must be light for comfortable casting. A

Captain Dave Markett often locates large snook like this one visually before presenting his bait or lure. He uses light tackle to fool the fish when the water is clear.

rod of this stiffness makes it possible to get the fish-attracting "pop" from these topwaters, the very quick splash and dart that turns snook on. It can't be done with a soft rod.

The stouter rod also makes it easier to muscle a big fish, though it takes some time to learn the limits of 8-pound test. The drag still has to be set light, at about 1/3 the breaking strength of the line, but you soon learn to use your finger to apply extra drag to the spool when you can get away with it, after the first big run is done and you're pumping the fish closer.

Wade-fishing can be a big help in getting close to hard-fished snook. The low profile and silent approach prevent spooking the fish. These anglers might do better, though, if they wore dark t-shirts.

Light, fast spinning gear is also nifty for working jigs and slow sinking plugs, and the sensitivity of the high-modulus graphite rods makes it easy to tell when a fish takes hold. Also, the stiffness of these rods transmits the hook set very directly, important when you're fishing thin line with a tendency to stretch considerably. Again, you have to learn just how much of a set the line will bear, but the skill comes quickly. (This gear is not suitable for Texas-rigged Jerkworms or Sluggos, however—it's too difficult to set the hook due to line stretch.)

THE HUNTER'S ARTS

When snook are lightly fished, they're no smarter than any other species. Any bait or lure that lands near them may bring the same sort of rush as rolling a bottle of Ripple into the drunk tank.

But when the fish get the sort of pressure they have for the last five years in most of Florida, anglers who consistently do well might want to adopt some of the skills of whitetail deer hunters to stalk and catch trophy snook.

SCOUTING

Scouting is the first and most important part of any deer hunt, and it's equally important when you go after hard-fished snook. If you don't know the terrain and how the quarry relates to it, success will be rare. The trick is not to accept what everyone else already knows and fish the "community holes" but to locate fish others have overlooked.

This means looking in unusual places: the boat basin that's carved up by a hundred outboards every weekend, the cleaning table at the end of a residential dock, the breakwater next to a crowded swimming beach, the deep water between a cruise ship and commercial docks.

Of course, learning to get into places others can't go is also a highly effective tactic—if you get a boat with an extremely shallow draft, it opens up tidal creeks along much of the west coast and throughout the Everglades where you won't find much company—but will sometimes find plenty of snook.

STALKING

Once you know where to look thanks to scouting, the stalk becomes important. Take another tip from good deer hunters: the quarry is just as sensitive to motion and sound as you'd be if you knew somebody were out to put a hit on you. Hey, it's not paranoia if somebody really IS trying to kill you! Don't assume snook are dumb enough to overlook your mistakes—don't give them anything to work with.

First, snook can often hear the approach of anglers long before they see them. Put your ear down in the water sometime in a busy fishing area and you'll hear outboards running 300 yards away. In areas where there are lots of boats running all the time, this is not a warning signal to fish. But in a backcountry creek, it will put them on red alert.

Solution? You have to go in without the outboard. Wading is by far the best approach — low profile, silent and very controlled. But it's slow and takes a lot of energy. If you're not close to a nice pod of fish, it can waste a lot of time.

The push pole is also a good choice—use it with the silence and delicacy of a bonefish guide and you'll spook few snook. (This means not banging it against the side of the boat or crunching it loudly into oyster shells, and no big, hard pushes when you're close to the fish. Just ease it along slightly faster than the wind drift for best results. And be ready to stake it in place quickly when a fish strikes.

Trolling motors are a distant third—they're good for getting within a hundred yards, but if you go much closer on hard-fished snook you'll set off the perimeter alarms. Some trollers run on their lowest speeds are nearly silent, and you can get a lot closer. But avoid bursts of high—they can be heard a long way underwater. And also avoid using a troller that has a damaged blade or bent shaft—these make a tremendous amount of underwater noise.

It's a good idea to mount your troller on a half-inch-thick foam rubber pad—this cuts vibration considerably. And remember, putting the troller into the operating position makes a lot of mechanical sounds—get it down before you get anywhere near the alleged hotspot.

Either poling or using an electric troller, you should also be aware of wave noise on the hull. Some hulls capture the little wavelets on the flats and magnify them into a very obvious sound, while others are nearly silent. Aluminum jon boats are bad about this, while a few of the best flats boats have designed the problem away. Test any boat you consider buying by easing it upwind and across wind in a light chop.

If your boat does tend to be noisy when poled upwind, you can avoid the problem by making only downwind approaches. This means you have to plan your attack to take advantage of the breeze, and maybe you don't fish some otherwise good spots at all until the wind is right. It's all part of the giant chess game that makes successful snooking so fascinating.

PRESENTATION

Not to mix metaphors, but if we can switch from hunting back to fishing for a moment, many snookers would benefit from lessons taught by expert brown trout anglers who fish in air-clear streams like some in central Pennsylvania or on the South Island of New Zealand. These guys will sometimes take 30 minutes to get into

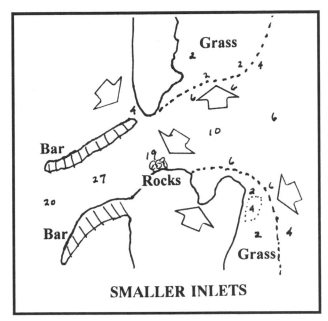

Grass

Bar

Rocks

Bar

Grass

SMALLER INLETS

Narrow spots like this always hold snook, but catching them requires a silent approach and a careful, planned cast. Fish are likely to be out on the points on rising water, dropping back to the cuts and channel edges as the tide falls.

position to make a single cast, and if that cast is delivered just right they catch the fish. If it's not, the game is over—they go on to look for another fish.

While we snookers don't have to be that cautious, if we put more thought into presentations, we'd catch more fish. The first cast is the money cast a lot of times when snook are under pressure, so it pays to do it right.

OK, let's assume you've made a good approach, silent and slow. The boat is slightly downcurrent and to the side of the spot so you can get a good drift without line drag. The sun is at your back so the fish is not going to look through his "window" and see the bad guy just outside. You've got on dark-colored clothes and your hull is a soft green or blue instead of a glaring white. You've gotten yourself up on the bow without kicking over the tacklebox. You're ready.

Or are you?

This is the time to stop and study the water a bit rather than whaling away with whatever happens to be tied on your leader.

If the fish are in a hole deeper than about 6 feet, you're probably not going to bring them up with a topwater. So you might tie on a slow-sinking plug — 52 M or the like — if the current is not really ripping through the hole, or a jig of appropriate weight if it is.

If you're fishing sardines or shrimp, you'd add a split shot to get the bait down. If the water is shallow, a topwater like the 7M or 28M is a good start. If there are lots of weeds or an overhang you're nervous about, a snagless soft-plastic bait, Texas-rigged, might be best.

Make sure the knots are good, clip the tag ends close and check your drag. You're ready to cast . . . or are you?

Not quite. Take a look at the way the water is moving. If it's boiling into the target zone, the fish probably are not going to be in there fighting it. They're likely to be off to one side where there's an eddy created by an oyster bar, mangrove limb or other obstruction.

Watch the way mangrove leaves drift through that eddy. In a lot of cases, you'll see there's actually a reverse current in along the shoreline, running in the opposite direction of the tide flow. The fish are likely to be tucked in there, their heads into that backwards flow. So, if you bring your lure in with the main current, it's approaching their tails, and they're not going to like that—baitfish don't mess with snook behinds if they know what's good for them.

There are several ways to tackle a spot like this. Maybe the first shot is to the edge of the current with a floater. You let the tide carry it down just past the end of the bar, then give it a few sharp twitches with the rod low, so that the current grabs the line and begins to pull the bait faster and faster downstream. If the fish are lying just off the flow, they're likely to attack.

If they're in the back-current, you may have to make a toss that actually lands downstream of the fish. In this case, you're going to keep the rod high and try to keep the line off the water—if you don't, the current is going to grab it and ruin the presentation. Let the bait drift a few yards upstream, then give it the sharp twitches to activate it across the eddy as it comes along the shoreline.

Two things to remember: Never let the lure land where you think the fish are holding — give them at least 10 feet in deep,

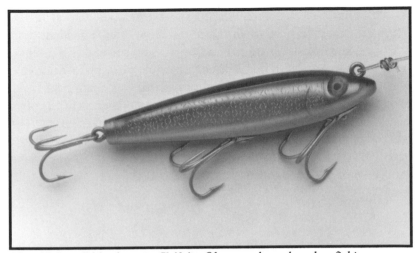

"Stealth lures" like the quiet 7M MirrOlure can be a plus when fishing nervous snook, particularly in shallow or calm water.

murky water and 30 feet in shallow, clear water. And secondly, the best presentation is the escape mode—if a lure swims toward them, they're going to get nervous. You want the lure trying to get away when it's just at the edge of their vision. This forces them to make a snap judgement—eat it or it disappears! A lot of times, they'll eat.

PRIME TIME

For lure-tossers, the early part of the open season can also be a bonanza time because pressure on snook has been minimal for the months during closure. Undisturbed fish are much more inclined to grab a darting piece of hard plastic than are those that have had the opportunity to learn the difference between every make and model.

And if you can get out after a week of bad weather, that's often prime time, too, because the fish will have had a chance to settle down and forget all the stuff that has been passing overhead. That's why Tuesdays, Wednesdays and Thursdays are usually better fishing than Friday through Monday. It's also part of the reason there's usually a good bite at dawn, and another one just before dark, after everyone has gone home to supper.

Of course, the fish feed best on the prime tides, the strongest outgoing flows. But, you fish when you have time. The ideal time, really, is when you've got a prime flow that comes at dawn or dusk, because then you've got the cover of minimal light to hide your mistakes. If you don't mind fishing at night, you'll do even better then for the same reason, as well as because there are no other boats out and because snook naturally like to feed at night. Just remember, they can satisfy their hunger in only a few minutes of active feeding, so being there at just the right time is important, especially if you're a lure-tosser.

CHAPTER 4

MAKING THEM EAT

OK, you know the water, you know which parts of it are likely snook habitat, you've learned how to put together the puzzle of tides to be in the right place at the right time, and you've gotten there without spooking the fish. Now you're faced with another dilemma. How do you make them bite?

While finding the snook is fully 75 percent of the battle, getting them to eat your lure or bait is the critical 25 percent without which the rest doesn't amount to a seagull's paintspot. (You know, the "paintspots" they make on your boat.)

First, you have to deliver the offering where it "ought" to be, according to the small but very precise brain of the alleged snook. Sardines don't fall out of the sky in the normal experience of most fish, and shrimp don't usually come with a 1-ounce anchor attached.

ACTIVE FISH

When snook are in a feeding mode, everybody is pointing more or less uptide in a flow-way, often around a point, a bridge piling, rockpile or other current-block that will allow the fish to hold position while they watch the tidal banquet flow by. There are eddies behind each of these areas, and the snook often lie in these because they don't have to exert any energy to stay put, yet they're just a tail-stroke from the chowline.

So, a good presentation is one that lands well upstream from this suspected congregation and brings the lure back down just a bit faster than the flow — just the way that mullet and sardines

Snook in clear water are the ultimate challenge. It takes a stealthy approach, accurate casts and light lines and leaders to fool them.

hurry ahead of the water, as if they're afraid it will leave them high and dry on the flats. When this delivery brings the bait around the tide-block and into view of the assembled fish, it often results in a bum's rush as everybody lunges for the goodies at once.

INACTIVE FISH

But, there are times when they're not that active — maybe the water is cold, or maybe somebody has already fished the spot that day, or maybe they fed all night and are full now — it happens, particularly on full-moon nights.

At these times, you have to spoon-feed them. Make a cast with a topwater like the 5M or 28M or a slow-sinker like a 52M and free-line it down with the current, allowing the whirl of the eddy behind the cover to actually pull the lure right into the lie. Then and only then, work it in very short but sharp twitches—move the rod tip just an inch or so, just enough to activate the lure, but not enough to move it out of the pocket. If they're in there, somebody will probably say "AH".

SEE WHAT YOU'RE LOOKING AT

And don't forget to see what you're looking at, as my old fishing uncle used to tell me. Some places where the tide is strong, there's actually a reverse current along seawalls and other cover, an area where the water appears to be running backwards for a considerable distance. Fish in that water will be facing toward this backflow. If you fish it in the usual way, you'll be bringing your lure to them tail-first.

They don't eat with that end, fellas.

Instead, make your cast close to the obstruction and work it with the backflow. In Nature's endless scheme of energy conservation, minnows don't swim upstream, at least not unless something is chasing them.

SINGLE FISH THAT CAN BE SEEN

Snook in a school are dummies compared to the single fish cruising alone, and snook in clear water are absolutely paranoid compared to those in water with a bit of color. Unfortunately, in the perverse way of all fishermen, many snookers consider sight-fishing for individual snook in air-clear water to be the ultimate thrill. It's definitely doing things the hard way to try to catch these fish, but when you pull it off it's a great triumph. Here are some tips gleaned from a few successes and thousands of failures.

First, of course, you have to make sure you see the snook and he doesn't see you. Snook often seem to be unaware that there's an angler within a mile when in fact they're watching every twitch of your rod out of the corner of their eye. They don't run off, they just go on alert and won't eat anything, sort of like zebras keeping an eye on the lion.

Dock snook are notorious for this, but fish on the flats also behave the same way. They can sense the mass of a boat coming through the water, they can hear a trolling motor running and they can feel the scrape of a push-pole against an oyster bar.

WADE THEM OUT

So you have to keep all this in mind and either make mega-casts or get out of your boat and down there with the stingrays for an amphibious assault.

Of course, it's Catch-22, because when you get down in the water, you can no longer see the fish unless they happen to be sitting on a white sand bottom at high noon on a sunny day, not something that snook generally like to do. But they can't see you, either, so you're on a level playing field . . . or at least one with only a few potholes.

The key to successful wading is to wear dark clothes and to keep it slow. Fish can spot a white tee-shirt a long way off, and they have learned since being hatched that white critters—gulls, egrets, Caucasians, etc.—are dangerous to their health. Wear something that blends with the mangroves and the grass, both above and below the water.

If you go fast enough that you push a bow wave, you will spook fish—and probably someday step on a stingray, too. Both for quiet and for safety, move slowly and do the flats anglers' favorite dance, the stingray shuffle. If you take only a couple slow steps at a time, you can actually walk up within 10 feet or so of many fish. Not that you'd want to—it's best to make the presentation as soon as the fish is in range of your best cast, so that there's less chance of scaring it off. And because there are always more fish that you don't see than fish that you do, you'll often get blind strikes by taking the slow approach and fan casting as you look for visible targets.

GETTING THE BITE

OK, all this is prologue — or foreplay for those of us who REALLY love snook fishing. Now, to making that individual fish bite: First, make the presentation as indicated above, with the tide. The best delivery to a visible fish is from slightly uptide and to one side. The cast should go upstream and a bit beyond the fish, so that it quarters back down as you retrieve, and slightly away from him, not directly at him. Avoid casting directly upstream over a fish's back, because it may spook from the fall of the line.

The idea is first to get the fish looking at the lure, which you can do by giving it a little "schlurp" as it lands—just a quick pull as it hits the surface makes it dart sideways and splash, sort of like baitfish do when they're startled. This is a lot more natural than the "plop" that baits make when falling straight down.

The fish may notice the bait right away, or he may not see it until it comes floating to him. In the best of all situations, you don't even have to think about it; he hits so fast that you don't see anything

A perfect presentation to a fish that's unaware of the angler usually results in a hookup. Waders do best with a very slow approach that gives them time to spot the fish—and also look for stingrays. (MirrOlure photo)

but a streak of bubbles. Snook can do that, striking faster than just about any inshore critter except a 'cuda.

WINDOW SHOPPERS

But more often you get an inspection: The fish may go on the alert, put out its fins and make a short sweep of the tail to point its nose at the bait, but not make any movement to attack. If it likes what it sees — the bait looks right and moves right — it may ease a bit closer.

Live bait can be a plus for catching wary fish in clear water. Change baits frequently; strikes come most often within the first minute after a fresh bait hits the water.

Don't freeze at this point. If the lure doesn't keep moving, the snook loses interest. Try to envision what you'd do if you were the alleged minnow and a piscavorous creature a hundred times your size were giving you the once-over.

Freako, right?

Translate that to the lure through your rod tip. Try for lots of lure action without too much forward motion—very short but very sharp twitches, increasing in intensity as the fish draws closer. As the fish starts to attack, increase the forward motion, as though it's making one final effort to outrun fate.

SPEED BALLS

If you make four or five deliveries to a fish and do all the shimmying and tantalizing possible to no avail, you might try the "speed ball". Use a vibrating lure like the 33 MR, wing a long cast well past the fish, and then bring it back at warp speed. Crank so fast that the lure is a blur.

Most of the time, this results in spooked fish. Occasionally, it results in catching snook that absolutely won't look at anything else, not even live baits.

Of course, the classic "Florida Whip" is also a high-speed retrieve, dancing the lure back and forth by nodding the rod tip up and down steadily as you wind steadily. It's tiring, but it has accounted for thousands of snook over the years.

FRESHEN YOUR BAITS

A sardine that has been on the hook 5 seconds has about 10 times the likelihood of getting eaten of one that has been on the hook 5 minutes. When a bait first hits the water it's frantic and full of energy, and all the action triggers even lethargic snook to strike. After the bait has been dragging the hook for a few minutes, it moves slower, flashes less and doesn't send out those frantic swimming vibrations, so it's attractiveness goes way down. Top snookers like Capt. Larry Mendez never fish a bait more than a couple of minutes, maybe two or three casts. Take the time to change baits frequently and you'll find yourself unhooking big snook a lot more frequently. (Of course, one of the advantages of artificials is they never get tired—at least not until your wrist wears out.)

DOUBLE THE BAITS DOUBLE THE FUN

Put two sardines on droppers about 18 inches apart and you drive snook nuts—they'll hit when they leave everything else alone. The two baits pull against each other in a mad, swirling dance that no gamefish can resist.

Of course, problems can arise if two fish decide to grab on at once—your leader usually parts. But this is a way to stir up lethargic fish when nothing else works.

OLD TRICKS

Also, don't forget the old tricks—a lot of them still work. MFC Commissioner Don Hansen, who has been a snooker for about six decades, still prefers a single-hook chrome spoon above all other lures, and catches loads of fish around his docks near Englewood with the lure night after night.

That same spoon cast back under the mangroves will catch plenty of fish. Advantage of the spoon is it allows a "skitter" cast, where you sidearm the lure hard and make it skip back under the overhanging limbs. This puts the bait several feet closer to the true shoreline, and right in the living room of the snook. It's deadly, particularly on hot summer days.

The old timers fishing the 10,000 Islands and the Everglades also caught plenty of snook by trolling sinking plugs and spoons in the murky waters there, and that's a tactic that's still worth trying for those who haven't found the hotspots. Trolling is less effective in the clearer waters up both coasts, but the murky jungle rivers here produce plenty of fish for trollers, and some of them are sizable.

CHAPTER 5

THE PASS MASTERS

It's more than a passing fancy.

From the full moon in May through the full moon in September, snook get moon-struck. It's the spawning time, and for those who don't mind catch-and-release fishing, it's also the best time of the year to tangle with a big linesider in any one of the passes of southern Florida.

The fish jam into these waters, pouring out of their usual haunts on the flats, shipping basins and bridges to form large "spawning aggregations" — sort of beach blanket bingo for fish.

The schools can be huge; experienced anglers estimate the school that forms each summer at Stump Pass near Englewood exceeds a thousand fish, and the spoil island at Port Manatee in Tampa Bay is thought to hold far more than that. Several schools of 100 fish or more prowl Jupiter and St. Lucie inlets throughout the summer, and most of these are big gals, 10 pounds and up.

The majority of the fish in these gatherings are 22 to 28 inches long, but there are some true bruisers in the mix as the largest females join the party. The summer spawn is the only time of the year when these giants, 20 pounds and up, are frequently encountered by anglers, and the high success rate on big fish was one of the reasons that the period had to be closed to harvest.

There's no rule against exercising the fish during the closed season, however, and with snook numbers currently at a modern high, it's pretty clear that release fishing is not harming the population.

Captain Scott Moore (right) is the acknowledged master of west coast passes. He spots pods of fish from his tower boat, then lures them with live sardines.

WHERE TO FIND THEM

The largest passes hold few snook in their main flow-ways, probably due to the lack of close-by seagrass nursery areas for the juveniles. Big waters like Egmont Channel and Boca Grande are not prime spawning areas. But the smaller cuts and passes that let off of these main flows are often super.

In a study conducted by Dr. Randy Edwards of Mote Marine a few years back, radio-tagged snook were found to stack up in the first small bay or cut inside major passes, rather than in the passes themselves. Thus, at Boca Grande, for example, while the main pass does not produce a lot of fish, go around the corner to the aging phosphate docks and you find monsters by the ton. The next dock up the way, the CSX recreational dock, also holds loads of fish. At St. Lucie, the fish find refuge behind a stone current break near the mouth of the pass, around the jetty tips, and in the approach channels but less often in the strong tides of the main flow itself.

And at the mouth of Tampa Bay, while Egmont and Southwest channels are not productive, the much smaller Passage Key Inlet is always loaded with fish in summer, particularly around the two fishing piers just inside Bean Point. And the pilot docks on the east side of Egmont Key, protected from the currents, often hold pickup trucks full of jumbo fish. Look for similar coves or protected areas around any pass close to you and chances are you'll find fish during summer.

WEST COAST PASSES

Most medium to small west coast passes hold lots of fish. Starting in the north, the action begins at the northern tip of Anclote Key, west of Tarpon Springs, where a deep cut goes through a sandbar. Other noted spots in this region include both ends of Three Rooker Bar, the north tip of Honeymoon Island, Clearwater Pass, Johns Pass, Blind Pass, Pass-A-Grille, and Bunce's Pass.

Moving south of Tampa Bay, Longboat, New Pass and Big Sarasota Pass are super summer snook spots. Venice Inlet produces giants around the jetties and along the riprap. Next comes the legendary Stump Pass, with top fishing in "Ski Alley". It's the narrow, northern arm of the inlet, and it's aptly named. Water skiers and jet skis buzz the place from dawn till dusk, yet it's alive with snook. Larger fish are often caught along the north beach at Stump after dark. Gasparilla Pass, the next inlet to the south, is just as good but gets much less pressure—check out the docks at the weekend homes on the north side, as well as the new piers at the very pricey new homes on the south.

Captiva Pass, at the south end of Cayo Costa Island, is always very good: fish stack up here at the grass edges on the north side and under the docks on the south side. Redfish Pass at the north tip of Captiva is a classic spot—tactic here is to drift with a live sardine

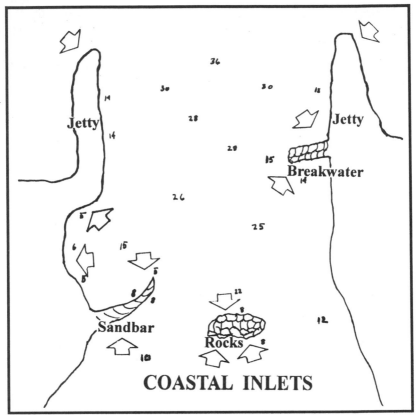

Snook don't often lie in the main current flow at a big inlet, but any breakwater, rockpile or bar that creates an eddy is likely to hold fish. Best time is usually on outgoing tide.

or pinfish just off bottom from the harbor entrance to the point on outgoing tide. There's also an excellent fishery around the corner on the south side, on the grass flat that lets off the entrance channel to the marina, and around the blown-down trees on the north side.

San Carlos Pass at the south tip of Sanibel is more a tarpon spot than a snook spot, but adjacent areas hold plenty of linesiders. The docks at Sanibel Harbour Resort, on the east side, are super, and there are sometimes pods along the edge of the broad flat on the south side of the causeway—an area that can be reached by wading.

Redfish Pass near Captiva Island is a classic spot for spawning snook. Anglers most often fish the outgoing tide here, dragging live pinfish close to bottom.

At Naples, Gordon Pass is excellent and both Little Marco and Big Marco are among the top producers in the state—drifting a live pinfish just off bottom is the killer tactic at Big Marco, but casting a black streamer fly on a sinking line from the beach at

Though summer is the best time of the year to catch large snook, the season is closed so all must be released. Studies by biologists indicate that nearly all fish released promptly survive.

night also gets plenty of fish. Caxambas, at the south tip of Marco, is also good.

In addition to these coastal passes, there are dozens of smaller passes that hold lots of fish in summer. The entrance alleys to Bull and Turtle bays off Charlotte Harbor are prime examples, as are the channels to Cockroach Bay and Bishops Harbor off Tampa Bay. In general, the main swash channel leading from a bayou into a larger bay is highly likely to hold fish.

For a rundown on prime east coast passes, see Chapter 15. The prime difference between east and west is that the spawn starts about a month later on the east side, but continues into September, which means if you're looking to harvest a few fish, these passes are a sure thing just after the fall season opens.

LOCATION, LOCATION, LOCATION

While it's well-known that snook pile up in the passes in summer, knowing exactly where they'll be on a given day separates the snookers from those who get snookered.

If possible, go at prime time — any of the three days before a new or full moon, when the majority of fish will be in the spawning mode. Biologists with the DEP have learned that the spawn is heaviest during these strong tide periods, probably because the flow helps move the fertilized eggs to the backwater habitat where they have the best chance of survival. At other phases, the fish will be around, but less concentrated and less eager to feed.

A typical pass may be 100 yards wide and 400 yards long, but the school of fish may cover a space not much larger than the average bedroom. It's not a needle in a haystack, but it can take some searching.

The first places to look are on any side bays or cuts just inside the main pass. A jetty or rock pile that breaks the current may be the key, or perhaps a large dock or a fallen tree. Most often you'll find them off to the side a bit where they don't have to fight the power of the strong, moon-driven tides.

TACTICS

The easy way to locate fish is with live chum. Toss a handful of dizzied, scaled sardines or threadfins into the flow, let them make a long drift down any suspect shorelines, and if they pass over snook the explosions will announce your discovery. To a lesser extent, live shrimp also work as live chum, though the fish sometimes suck them in without the surface commotion that's common when chasing sardines. A noisy topwater worked fast will also draw them up — try a chugger like the 88 MR or a prop bait like the 5M.

You can also try sight fishing. When the sun is high and the water is clear, you can sometimes see the schools—they appear as a dark green or gray mass over the lighter green of the sand bottom in most passes. You need polarized glasses, of course, and the higher above the water you can get, the better your chances of seeing the fish—that's why the half-towers are so popular with flats guides these days.

STRUTTING SNOOK

There are times when the snook make it easy. Occasionally you'll see a fish, decked in the bright yellow fins of the spawning period, displaying at the surface. They swim along slowly, almost drunkenly, the dorsal fin and part of the tail out of water. Why?

Hard to say, but my theory is that they are "strutting", or advertising for mates—it's a behavior familiar to any wild turkey hunter.

Fish that are swimming this way don't often bite, but you can be sure that there are plenty of other fish close by when you see one cruising this way.

PRESENTATION

When it comes to artificials, the presentation seems to be as much the key to success as lure choice. A 1/4 to 1/2 ounce jig with a 4-inch plastic swimmer tail is a dependable producer almost anywhere. Also good are slow-sinking plugs like the 52M, 38M and 33M MirrOlure. And soft plastic DOA shrimp and mullet are also very effective.

The fish in the passes always nose into the tide, and they feed most often on the fall, when all the bait on the flat funnels through the deep water of the channel.

The secret to success with artificials is to position yourself slightly downtide of the fish and cast uptide, beyond them, then allow the current to sweep the bait through them as you slightly activate it. When the lure stops, you set the hook.

On the casts where you don't get a hit, you reel in and cast uptide again. Importantly, live baits are fished the same as artificials here—letting them hang in the tide rarely succeeds.

BEACHING

Pre- and post-spawn snook often prowl the beaches, particularly within a couple hundred yards either side of the passes. The fish along the beach more often feed on rising water, when the incoming tide allows them to get at fiddlers and other crustaceans along the sand. (Snook love crabs—Captain Scott Moore notes that virtually every snook he's ever cleaned has had crab shell among the stomach contents. They're an overlooked and very hardy bait.)

For beach fish, the trick is to keep your casts fairly close to the shore as you stroll along the break—casting straight out is less productive, usually, than landing your offering within 20 feet of the sand. Make long casts to avoid the fish seeing you in the clear water, but make them parallel to the shore. Topwater plugs often do well in the shallow water here, and fishing is always better after

If you decide to hold a fish up for pictures, don't depend on the jaw alone to support it. A better approach is to take the jaw grip with the left hand, and use the right hand to support the tail.

dark. Surf fishing is usually best during calm periods when the water is not turned milky by sand.

ETHICS OF FISHING THE SPAWN

Should the spawning season be closed to all snook fishing, even catch-and-release? Some anglers say it should because capture disturbs the spawning cycle and results in some mortality among released fish. But according to the state's lead snook scientist, Ron Taylor of the Florida Marine Research Labs in St. Petersburg, catch-and-release fishing does not cause much mortality in the species.

It's likely that nearly all fish that are not deeply hooked and that are released after a quick photo do survive. Whether or not the shock of being caught upsets the spawning cycle is another matter. Studies at Mote Marine Labs in Sarasota seem to indicate that fish captured and held absorb their eggs and do not spawn, but whether that occurs in fish released back into their own habitat is not known.

However, the overall abundance of the species seems to indicate that there is no shortage of successful egg fertilizations.

If you choose to fish during the spawn, pay special attention to releasing the fish quickly and carefully. The best release is one that does not lift the fish from the water; use pliers and simply flip the hook free. Bend down the barbs on all your hooks so that they'll come out easily.

And if you decide to hold a fish up for pictures, don't depend on the jaw alone to support it. (Snook tend to flop wildly when grabbed by the jaw anyway.) A better approach is to take the jaw grip with the left hand, and use the right hand to support the tail. With a wet hand, grip the body behind the anal fin where there are no internal organs. Bend the body slightly to the side and the fish won't flop, making it safer for you and the snook.

Remember, the fish is not getting much oxygen while he's out of the water, yet he needs it desperately because he's just worn himself out fighting the line. Sort of like you'd feel if you ran a hundred yards and then stuck your head in a bucket of water. How long could you hold your breath in that situation? Make the photo quickly and get the fish back into the water, and your summer catches won't create problems for the fish we all love.

CHAPTER 6

MASTERS OF DARKNESS

The midnight ramblers prowl the darkness.

They're dangerous-looking men, red-eyed, bristle-faced, dressed in camouflage and armed with what has to be described as assault gear, the heavy weaponry of the snooking game.

THE MAD SNOOKER

Anglers like Dave Pomerleau, the self-proclaimed "Mad-Snooker" of the west coast, become strangers to daylight. Because snook usually bite better after dark, many snook-o-philes confine their forays to the hours between sundown and sunrise, to the detriment of families, jobs and normal REM patterns.

Pomerleau, who considers any night he doesn't tangle with at least 30 linesiders a complete bust, has been at the game so long he doesn't mind fishing in the dark—in fact, he prefers it.

"The fish always bite better after sundown," says Pomerleau. "That's their nature. And, when it's late, all the other anglers go home so the fish aren't disturbed."

Pomerleau and other after-dark experts concentrate on the "light line" where bridge lights create a sharp edge between light and darkness. They routinely make catches that would amaze daytime fishermen, all without ever stepping into a boat.

Pomerleau even built a special bait trailer to tote his 500- pound live well, a custom-made fiberglass rig designed to keep a dozen foot-long mullet alive. And his night-time forays sometimes begin in St. Petersburg and end in Naples.

Captain Dave Pomerleau got this awesome monster on one of his night forays along Florida's west coast. The giant taped 49 inches long. It grabbed a foot-long ladyfish under a bridge.

"I just keep driving, trying new bridges, until I find one where the fish are turned on," says Pomerleau. "I know that on any night, the fish are going to be really hot at one of these spots, and all I have to do is find it."

Dave Pomerleau finally broke down and got himself a flats boat after he went into the guide business, but his heart is still up there on the catwalk anytime the sun goes down.

SNOOK JUSTICE

In a sport where one lunker a lifetime is considered a gift, Dave Justice breaks the mold. He may be the all-time champion at catching monster snook. The former Miamian can account for more than 500 fish over 30 pounds!

Of course, it took Justice almost 20 years of fishing to compile this score, but catching so many true monster snook would be an astonishing achievement in a 100-year span. In fact, most anglers never land even one linesider of such heroic dimensions.

It helped that Justice grew up in southeast Florida, fishing mostly the waters between Biscayne Bay and Fort Pierce—the area where Florida snook reach the largest sizes.

He also spent countless hours on the water after dark, the time when the lunkers prowl. But he attributes most of his success to targeting big fish and only big fish.

"It's a matter of fishing where the biggest snook live with big baits and with tackle heavy enough to land them when they bite," Justice says. "I don't bother with areas that I know hold only fish under 15 pounds and I don't mess with light tackle."

Indeed he does not. His main live bait rod is a custom-built monstrosity 9 1/2 feet long with a handle almost three inches thick and three feet long. The reel is a 4/0 Penn with a customized drag system. Line is 80-pound-test mono, leader 130-pound test mono, and the hooks would handle Jaws—they're 9/0 forged Mustads.

Justice's baits are equally impressive—like Dave Pomerleau, when he's after giant fish, a 1 1/2 pound mullet, ladyfish or croaker or a 3/4-pound mojarra or grunt are typical offerings. Big diving plugs also get the nod.

Where to find the lunkers? Usually in big water with lots of bait and lots of current.

"You might see a rare individual female over 20 pounds back on the flats, but as a rule the big fish are going to be in the ocean and gulf passes or around the bridges on the intracoastal waterway." Justice says. "It's not their nature to live up in the shallows."

He notes that in winter some big fish move to the powerplants, and some work well inland to find warm water, but the big fish feed less and are not as easy to catch at that time. His favorite months are April through October when the fish are most active and nearer the coast.

He prefers to fish inlets from a boat, drifting his baits with the current or trolling plugs deep, then motoring back uptide for another drift. He pays particular attention to jetties or bars that create eddies where the snook can hold just out of the strongest current flow.

He also likes to fish bridges over passes and other major channels, and he often works these from the span overhead.

East Coast fish bite just as well after sundown. This nice one came from St. Lucie Inlet near Stuart. It grabbed a soft-plastic mullet drifted near bottom on falling tide.

"A lot of times, the fish will be on the shadow-line created by overhead lights on the uptide side of the bridge, because that's where they get first crack at bait coming through with the flow," he says. "I always try that first, and if that doesn't work I'll work the downtide side."

With his heavy gear, he sometimes allows his baits to drift under the bridge from the uptide side, depending on the power of the tackle to yank the fish back through under the bridge if he gets a strike.

"The extra long rod gives you a big advantage on a bridge because it lets you keep the line below the road bed. When a fish hits, you've got to have that length so that you don't get cut off on the cement."

He said that fish tend to gather in particular spots on particular bridges, and will show up within 10 feet of those same spots year after year.

Captain John Griffith of Tampa scores after dark by timing his trips to the strongest tide flows. He likes to skip live shrimp under residential docks to lure out hiding lunkers.

"It takes a lot of time getting to know your area, but once you get it scoped out you can spend your time with the bait always in the strike zone," Justice says. He locates his spots by counting pilings.

His all-time best was a 42-pounder that taped 49 inches long. That fish, like 95 percent of the others he has caught, was released to fight again.

David Justice's tactics are detailed in his 75-minute video, "Successful Snook Tactics". The video includes some unique underwater footage of free-swimming snook as well as lots of fishing action. It's $24.95 from High Hook, 9930 NW 59th Court, Parkland, FL 33076, (800) 340-1544.

BRIGHT LIGHTS, BIG CITIES

Though snooking is often associated with mangrove wilderness, some of the best night snooking takes place around major metropolitan centers. The more traffic, the more bridges, and the more bridges over deep water, the more snook.

However, experienced night fishermen say that the mistake many anglers make is quitting too soon in their night forays.

"It takes an hour or two of black dark before the fish really get going on most lights," says Capt. John Griffith of Tampa. "and if the tide isn't moving then, they may wait until it is."

Griffith catches fish by the dozens by working quietly around residential docks and bridges in St. Petersburg on his trolling motor, pitching live shrimp under the structure.

"The fish you can see are hard to catch," he advises. "Try the edge of the shadow, where you can't see them, and you'll usually get bites right away. Sometimes you have to skip the bait back under the dock to make it happen."

Though nearly every night of the year can produce good snook fishing, best action is on those with strong tide flows. Time the trip to hit the peak flows. Why fish from 8 p.m. until midnight if the tide doesn't get right until 1 a.m. Better to sleep until midnight and then go fishing.

It all results in a lot of red eyes and questioning spouses, but for really serious snookers, night-stalking is well worth while.

CHAPTER 7

SNOOKING BY THE SEASONS

Face it, the best time to go snook fishing is after the season closes.

In fact, the reason the Florida snook season is closed from June through August is that the fishing is too good during these months— biologists discovered in the 1970's that up to 70 percent of the annual snook catch was being taken in summer, and that harvest was depleting the species. The summer spawn fishing is detailed in Chapter 5. But for many, closed season fishing lacks something — snook fillets.

POST SPAWN PATTERNS IN FALL

The question when the season re-opens on September 1 usually is: where did all those spawners go?

Undoubtedly, there will be some stragglers left around the passes, but the majority are gone on the west coast. On the east coast the spawn runs nearly a month later, but the fish are gone from the passes by the time the first of the mullet run arrives on October 10 or thereabout.

Some go to the beach. The classic action of early fall is along the sand as big schools of the fish move out to cruise the surf, feeding on sardines and glass minnows on the west coast, mullet on the east.

Fish that spawn in inside areas don't travel all the way to the outside beaches, of course—most simply slide off to the nearby flats to feed.

Fishing along the beaches usually picks up as the spawn ends. Fish that were in the passes cruise the surf looking for food. Most are found in the swash channel inside the first bar.

And a lot of snook will again take up residence under the bridges, piers and docks where they spend much of the year, feeding heavily after dark, loafing in the depths like lazy sharks during daylight.

The trick in fall is to keep moving until you locate a concentration, rather than exhaustively working a limited spot to try to make it produce.

There's often a transition period, ranging from a week to a month or more, when the fish are staging in the river mouths and nearby flats, and this can often provide very hot action because a lot of snook are crowded into pretty tight areas, much as in spring when they first come out on the flats.

BACKCOUNTRY LINESIDERS

Snook that spawn on the inside passes tend to remain near those passes after the mating season ends. This means that areas like the flats south of Tampa Bay's Port Manatee are likely, as are those south of the Bishop's Harbor entrance and around Joe Island. Also in Tampa Bay, check out Miguel Bay and Rattlesnake Key near the mouth of the Manatee River. On the north side of Tampa Bay, the Weedon Island flats are likely to have fish—smart, but catchable on live sardines and on stealth baits like the 28M.

Charlotte Harbor usually has plenty of fish on the inside as well. Areas that usually have backcountry fish on opening day include the islands inside Captiva Pass in Pine Island Sound, those north and south of the Burnt Store channel on the east side of the harbor, and the bars south of the Bull Bay/Turtle Bay island chain.

WINTER SNOOKING

The winter snook season starts with a bang as hundreds of fish pour into the rivers over a few days, usually after the first front in mid-October or early November when water on the flats drops below 68 degrees. After that, things gradually slow down as the water gets progressively colder until fishing pretty much comes to a stop by early January and stays dead until the warm days of early March. Chilly waters slow the metabolism of fish in most refuge areas, strong winds make it tough to control the boat and the cold makes things just plain uncomfortable for anglers a good portion of the days.

But, we're snookers and we must go snook fishing. Classic winter snook water is found in the larger rivers and deep creeks, where black water absorbs more heat than the clear water in the bays at this time of year. Powerplant outflows also hold fish but because these fish get lots of pressure, it's tough to catch them without live bait, preferably fished after sundown.

There are also fair numbers of fish in the residential canals inside the barrier islands throughout snook country. Again, these fish bite best after sundown, with a large, live shrimp or slow-sinking plug the most successful offering. They're easiest to find by fishing dock lights, where they often lie just below the surface. However,

When winter comes, bay snook often cruise into coastal rivers and travel miles upstream seeking warm water. Captain Dave Markett finds lots of nice ones in the Anclote River.

wind and rain, which turn these canals murky, often put the fish off their feed for several days at a time throughout the winter.

The river fish will take topwater plugs fished along the mangrove edges with some regularity, but the fish on the shores are likely to be small ones, less than the minimum 24 inches. Bigger fish come from the deep holes and from the canals, and are usually caught on sinking plugs, live shrimp, tilapia, pinfish or freshwater shiners.

And, yes, snook do swim all the way into fresh water as they proceed upstream in coastal rivers. They're caught along the east shore of Lake Okeechobee with some regularity, 60 to 100 miles from the nearest saltwater. In many coastal rivers, it's common to catch a snook on one cast and a largemouth bass on the next from November through March.

The snook tend to settle in deep river bends, dredge holes and around bridge abutments, and also sometimes prowl creek mouths when falling tides pull bait to them there. It's interesting fishing, productive even when strong winter winds would make fishing open bays impossible.

There are also fair numbers of snook that head to offshore reefs and wrecks when it gets uncomfortably cold inshore. Artificial reefs off Fort Myers and the natural ledges off Stuart hold hundreds of fish some winters.

RITES OF SPRING

As spring approaches, the first warm days are greeted by all cold-blooded creatures with an urge to warm up by sunning, and snook take advantage of the heat just as garter snakes and gila monsters do. In fact, the current fly-rod record snook in the 20-pound tippet, 30 pounds, 2 ounces, by angler Rex Garret and guide Pete Vilano, was taken in about a foot of water in an Everglades creek on just such a morning. See the chapter on fly fishing for the details.

Once the spring migration is on, fish move to the beaches and main bay shorelines where the early runs of baitfish will appear. They also hang around river mouths and the nearest flats to these outflows about the time the water temperature passes 72 degrees.

For anglers with boats, beach fishing is a matter of running the slough, the channel that makes up inside the first bar along the beach, until you see fish flushing ahead of the boat. This is best done between 10 a.m. and noon, when the high sun will help you see into the water, and also when the afternoon westerly wind will not yet have made the trough too rough to run on many days. If there's much more than a gentle swell, you can't see the fish, and the surf is too rough to stop and fish in any case.

When you do see fish, turn back, give them five minutes to settle down, and then ease in on trolling motor or push pole. Topwaters, slow sinkers, jigs and live sardines all work well. ("Rallying" the fish like this works OK on the beach, where they're less spooky, but avoid it on the grass flats — you're likely to run them completely out of your fishing area.)

Captain Pete Greenan tussles with a linesider at Charlotte Harbor. In spring, snook that wintered in holes and rivers of the backcountry head for the flats to feed. They're good targets for artificials at this time of year.

When the surf is dead calm, as it sometimes is on summer mornings, it's no problem to work along the beach as you would a mangrove shoreline, casting ahead as the boat is controlled with a trolling motor. If there's much wave action, it's better to drop anchor, bow to the waves, and let the stern drift back to within casting range of the fish.

Anglers who fish from the beach sometimes do better than those in boats because they're not so affected by the swells, and also because they can better run their baits parallel to the surfline, where the fish often look for food. Too, in the clear water, the minimal profile of a wading angler is much less evident to the fish than the hull of a boat.

In spring, snook move back to river mouths, along the beaches and to the flats to greet the arrival of the whitebait runs into the warming waters. The first few days after fish leave the rivers can offer phenomenal fishing, as proven here by Capt. Mel Berman, well-known radio host from Tampa.

Fishing along the beaches is usually a rising tide proposition as the fish cruise the break-line looking for crabs and minnows. Areas that are particularly productive are often the first 200 yards on either side of a pass, around concrete groins placed to prevent beach erosion — much of the beach at Boca Grande is an example — and "run-outs" where the wash of the surf creates gullies in the beach. There are many very strong runouts in the heavy surf of the Atlantic beach, and those near the major snook passes often hold fish.

Most passes have secondary passes cut through the main bars that make up along the deepest part of the channel, and these smaller passes are often the place to find a load of snook. Fish them on falling water when all the baitfish on the inside will funnel through. These cuts are often at the point where the main bar along the edge of the pass heads seaward. The channel will be within 50 feet of the beach, and it may not be all that obvious, perhaps only a foot or two deeper than the rest of the bar. But a lot of current goes through these cuts, and they often produce, particularly after sundown when the fish feel more secure in the shallow, clear water.

Along the beach, the fish may be anywhere from the first bar to right up against the shore, but they're not very often beyond the bar. You'll see some enthusiasts wade out chest deep and then bust their BVD's to throw another 200 feet seaward, but these guys are usually fishing behind the snook. The action is likely to be within 50 feet of where the water hits the sand, so casts that work parallel to the beach and out to water about 4 feet deep are most likely to be effective.

In all beach areas, remember that the predominate baitfish are pale silver in color. Lures with light green backs and silver sides are likely to do best. A silver spoon can also be effective, as is a silver-flake swimmer tail jig about 3 to 4 inches long.

The fish tend to come out of the rivers on the first warm days of late March or early April—you can tell, because it will be a time when you want to play hooky from work, a couple of unusually warm, calm days with the scent of new flowers blooming and the bees buzzing. It's Nature's wake-up call, and the fish feel it just as we do. By staying alert for these signals of the changing seasons, master snookers can stay on the fish movements pretty much year around.

CHAPTER 8

MANAGING FOR TOMORROW

Modern snook management has come about in halting steps, with the managers for the most part one step behind the fish population in the early years. Recent efforts concentrating more on conservation than on public pressures have done better. And the applied research done since funding arrived through the snook stamp has provided quantum leaps.

Snook had no management at all through 1947, and up until that time an estimated 1.25 million pounds per year were taken in nets. Gill and trammel nets were banned for the species in '47, followed by a ban on haul seines in 1951, the same year in which the first size limit, 18 inches, was put in place for recreational anglers.

A four-fish bag limit was established in 1957 and sale was prohibited. But all these regulations didn't restore the fish. By the late 70's, researchers lead by Jerry Brueger from the Department of Environmental Protection discovered nearly all the spawners were being caught out of the passes of southwest Florida. Based on their reports, a two-fish limit was put in place in 1981, followed by a June/July closure in 1982, and the January/February closure in 1983.

August was added to the summer closure in 1985, and at the same time the 24"-34" slot limit was put in place, with one fish over 34" allowed daily.

In 1994 the winter closure was adjusted to Dec. 15-Jan. 31— just in time for a hard February freeze in 1995. Thus, snook went

Should we release more snook so that more can attain trophy size? Some anglers would rather have snook fillets, while others already consider linesiders a catch-and-release trophy like tarpon.

from no-holds-barred to being the most tightly regulated fish in Florida over a 50-year period. One has to wonder if the restoration could have been accomplished much sooner had the stouter measures been taken 20 years ago, but hindsight is always 100 percent.

FUTURE MANAGEMENT

Ron Taylor, the DEP biologist who rides herd on snook from the Marine Lab in St. Petersburg, submitted a report to the MFC in 1993 outlining the effect a one-fish limit would probably have on the species.

According to Taylor, plenty of snook survive to spawning age on both coasts, with 38 percent reaching that age on the west coast of Florida, and maybe a few more on the east coast.

An interesting bit of anecdotal data, as the biologists call reports from anglers: captains Van Hubbard and Scott Moore, who fished the summer spawning aggregations in the passes along the west coast, reported in the summer of 1996 that their catches were approaching an all-time high in numbers, with both skippers guiding their parties to more than 100 fish on some days. However, only about 10 percent of those fish were 24 inches long or larger—quite a bit under the 38 percent predicted by the biological models.

If the limit were reduced to one fish, Taylor estimated that the harvest would be reduced 16 percent on the west coast, 6 percent on the east coast. That would result in a 3 percent increase in the numbers of adult fish on the west coast, and a 10 percent increase in adults on the east coast.

Biologists generally view any fish population where 35 percent of the individuals reach spawning age as a healthy population. So why tinker with the limits to raise the snook stocks so far above that line?

Taylor notes that snook are a delicate species subject to sudden drops in population due to winter-kill. Dr. Russ Nelson, executive director of the MFC and also a marine biologist, has suggested that a cushion of added spawners, at a minimum 40 to 45 percent of the total stocks, be maintained to protect against a population crash caused by cold weather.

Taylor has also suggested elimination of the "one-fish-over 34-inches" rule, should a one-fish bag limit ever be put in place.

"If you want to protect these big fish, which are the most productive spawners, you need to eliminate them from the harvest," says Taylor. "A one-fish limit with no upper size limit would in effect allow the same number of the largest to be harvested as under the present rules."

Taylor also suggests that the closed winter season has not been particularly effective at protecting fish. His studies show that the harvest reduction of spawners via the closure in January and February is less than 1 percent on either coast. Catch rates, as indicated by tag returns, were at a yearly low from December through March on the east coast, so Taylor thinks that opening the winter months would not result in a significant catch increase. (Of course, it's possible that people don't fish for snook during the closed seasons because they can't keep them, and would fish them heavily if they could.)

Captain Richard Knox shows a doubleheader taken near Tarpon Springs. Big, healthy fish like these are prime spawning stock. Knox and other guides encourage releasing them and keeping smaller fish.

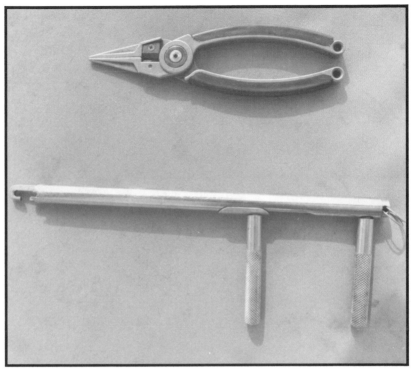

Successful release requires sturdy tools for prompt hook-removal. The best release is one in which the fish is left in the water while the hook is popped out.

Whether or not we tinker with the snook regulations is mostly a matter of philosophy, according to Taylor, who agrees that current regulations appear to be working well.

"If we want to eat fish, then we should keep it at two fish," Taylor said. "If we want to catch more fish and bigger fish, then a one-fish limit would probably help that happen."

One point not considerd is the impact on trophy fishermen, who might want to collect a record fish. If the one-over-34-inches rule is dropped, it would be impossible to keep a new world record, just as it is now impossible to keep a record redfish. (Record fish can be weighed on certified scales, photographed and then released according to IGFA rules, however.)

It would make sense, it seems, to adopt a rule similar to that applied to tarpon, where special tags are required. A system allowing a single oversized fish each year via a permit or tag would work well for snook. Since snook tags are already required to harvest any size of snook, it would be a simple matter to add a detachable trophy-fish tag to the stamp.

Once used, no further large fish could be collected until the next year's stamp was purchased. A system like this is used effectively for western steelhead and for Texas redfish, among other species. It costs the angler nothing extra, but serves as a check on excessive harvest of the largest fish. And the tag returns would add one more bit of information to the puzzle for biologists and fishery commissioners attempting to manage snook populations.

CHAPTER 9

SEA GRASSES
NURSERY OF THE FLATS

There's not much that's more beautiful to the eye of a snooker than a rich turtle grass flat stretching away through clear, knee-deep water to a distant wall of mangroves. The ribbon-like strands of gray-green vegetation are a welcome sign to fish and fishermen, a nursery for young fish as well as a feeding station for the adults. And a healthy grass flat is a sure sign of excellent water quality.

But we may be loving our sea grass flats to death.

According to a study by scientists with the Florida Marine Research Lab in St. Petersburg (the research arm of the Department of Environmental Protection), many grassy shallows around the state are now being damaged by powerboats.

Tampa Bay is one area where damage is common according to the report. Others are Charlotte Harbor, the Florida Keys, and the flats of Citrus and Levy counties.

What have all these areas in common?

Flats boats, and until July of 1995, gill net boats.

It was ironic that these two adversaries were in the same boat, so to speak, when it came to damaging the habitat where they spend most of their time on the water. Most of the net boats are gone now, but for every well-boat that went away, three or four new flats boats appeared, and many net fishermen now travel the same areas tossing castnets or running crab traps

The damage comes not from the hulls but from the props, which scour the bottom and uproot weeds when the boats run through water that's too shallow—depths ranging from 6 inches to 3 feet are getting hurt the worst.

Grouper fishermen don't run in water this shallow. Neither do mackerel fishermen. The damage is being done mostly by the growing army of flats anglers in pursuit of snook, redfish and trout, as well as permit and bonefish in the Keys, plus the inshore commercial guys.

It has been standard operating procedure for years for flats boats to run these waters with at least the skeg touching bottom, and in soft bottom like that found in the Keys, flats fishermen regularly blow over shoals with the prop half-way buried in the marl. Commercial well-boats run with the prop in a tunnel and don't touch bottom in depths less than a foot, but since they run shallower areas, they do their share of damage.

When there were not more than 200 flats boats in the whole state, this was not much of a problem. Now that there are thousands, it is becoming a big problem—and one that may result in regulations that put a lot of these prime fishing waters off limits to operation under power. Like the old saying goes, we have met the enemy, and he is us!

The researchers compiled their study based on aerial photos as well as on-water observation. They say that some 2,500 acres of grass are severely damaged in Tampa Bay. An area was considered "severely damaged" if more than 20 percent of the given flat bore prop scars.

Of course, a scar on a seagrass flat is not the same thing as a scar on a manatee. A few prop cuts through a flat do no damage to the overall productivity of that habitat, and in fact, the deeper strips created in broad shallow areas may be helpful in fish production, though purist environmental types don't like to hear that fact. As every flats fisherman knows, on low tide snook and reds frequently settle into the cuts created by just such scarring.

But problems arise when so many boats buzz an area that broad swaths of grass are uprooted and wide channels cut. The grass takes

Turtle-grass flats are nurseries for snook, as they are for many other inshore species. However, flats boats are damaging the grass in some high-traffic areas.

years to regrow, and the turbidity or murkiness caused by the whirling props reduces light penetration into the water, slowing the spread and regrowth of the grass. Too much turbidity can actually kill healthy sea grass. It's a vicious circle which, if repeated too often, can result in destruction of large areas of the flats.

A second problem is the disturbance of "sheet flow", that is the flow of water over shallows that are only inches deep. When a deeper channel is opened up, most of the water rushes through that cut, and the tidal interchange over the shallow areas is reduced. Clean, oxygenated water is not brought in, and nutrified water is not carried out. The mixing that makes an estuary function is reduced.

Shallow-draft tunnel-hulls like the author's Hydra-Skiff can operate with the prop actually above the bottom of the hull, greatly reducing grass damage. The tower is a help in avoiding areas that are too shallow for safe operation as well as in spotting fish.

WHO DONE IT?

To a considerable extent, the flats boat industry and those of us who write about it are at fault because we have touted boats that run in 12 inches, 10 inches, even 8 inches of water.

In fact, a boat with a 14-inch diameter prop can't run in water that's 8 inches deep and have the skeg completely clear the bottom. What these boats actually do is skim along with the lower blade of the prop and the skeg touching the thin mix of sand and mud that makes up the top few inches of the bottom. The boat travels effectively through the shallows, but it leaves a trail in doing so. That trail causes no problem on a bare bottom, but on grass it leaves a mark that will be a long time in healing.

In Tampa Bay, the problem is particularly acute. The bay is in a recovery cycle with sea grasses beginning to grow in areas where they have not been seen in decades thanks to the clean-up of water quality as a result of the S.W.I.M. and Agency for Bay Management

In the future, one of the signs of a master snook fisherman may be that he or she realizes how closely good fishing is tied to good habitat, and does his or her part to protect and preserve that habitat.

efforts as well as better sewage treatment. But the grass can't come back in high-traffic areas until the prop scarring stops.

Sarasota Bay and Terra Ceia Bay have problems similar to Tampa Bay. And Charlotte Harbor, though in better health, is now being inundated with waves of new flats boats. The same is true in the Indian River, Banana River and Mosquito Lagoon on the east coast.

All of this will have to stop. It will stop either as a result of sport fishermen agreeing to stop running the flats in areas that are too shallow for bottom clearance, or it will stop when government agencies kick us off the flats.

The study by the Research Lab was turned over to regulatory agencies. At Tampa Bay, waters around Weedon Island and Fort DeSoto have already been put off limits to operation with motors, and access to Cockroach Bay has been severely limited to those running outboards. Access by push pole remains legal, but there's no more skimming the flats in these areas. Other areas of the state are seeing similar regulations. Ironically, the excessively harsh boating rules pitched to save manatees may now be needed to save the flats themselves.

Unfortunately, a lot more of this is in our future, and we have mostly ourselves to blame. We enjoyed a good thing a bit too much. In the future, one of the signs of a master snook fisherman may be that he or she realizes how closely good fishing is tied to good habitat, and does his or her part to protect and preserve that habitat.

CHAPTER 10

MASTERING ARTIFICIAL LURES

There's no doubt a good lure fisherman could catch plenty of snook with a 6-inch piece of shovel handle rigged with a couple of treble hooks. It ain't how it looks, but how it moves that matters, and 90 percent of how it moves depends on the angler rather than the lure.

However, there are some lures that make it a lot easier to do it right, and a few that have proven themselves classic snook-catchers for decades.

Many companies make good snook lures, and I've fished most of them over the years. L & S Baits in Largo, Florida, manufacturer of MirrOlures, has kindly agreed to help sponsor this book, so we'll take a close look at their product line here. It's probably safe to say that more snook have been caught on MirrOlures than all others combined.

Harold LeMaster brought the company to Florida in 1948, and since that time the "lures with the built-in flash" have become the favorite of generations of snookers. The company is headed by Harold's son Bill today, and has branched out to offer a remarkable selection of lures: 45 body styles and 31 color combinations.

THE SNOOKER'S TACKLEBOX

Among the topwaters, every serious snooker's tacklebox should include the 7M and 28M MirrOlures which are basic "twitchbaits", the shiner-imitating 32M Glad-Shad, the 5M which is a prop bait, the 12M, 44M and 85M poppers, and the 95M and 97M stickbaits.

Snook feed primarily on small baitfish, which is why minnow-imitating lures work so well for them. There are times when plugs readily out-fish live bait.

Each of these lures has its own best time and place. The twitchbaits are the top choice in calm, clear or very shallow water because they create less disturbance than some lures and are less likely to spook fish. Prop baits and poppers are much more aggressive lures capable of attracting fish with sound, so they work best when water is rough, murky or deep, and also after dark.

Captain Mark Bennett, a MirrOlure pro-staffer, says the stickbaits are especially effective for probing out new areas rapidly because they can be fished very fast without losing their attraction. Since the weight is in the tail of the lure, they're also the best-casting of all MirrOlures. The lure never dives, making it good to use in areas where grass is within inches of the surface.

SLOW-SINKERS

While topwaters are the most fun to fish, the deadliest of all snook plugs is probably the slow-sinker like the classic 52M, the 38M and 33MR and the TT series. These lures can be fished anywhere from the surface down to about 8 feet, but the deeper you

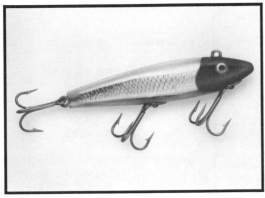

The 52M MirrOlure is one of the classic snook plugs. The slow-sinking lure can be fished effectively at depths from 6 inches to 5 feet, covering most of the range where snook are found year-around.

want to fish them the slower you must fish them. They're ideal spring and summer baits when the fish are in water 1 to 3 feet deep, particularly the 51M, a shallower-running cousin of the 52M. But all continue to be effective in winter with a slower retrieve as they sink down 4 to 8 feet.

FAST-SINKERS

L & S also makes some heavily weighted plugs designed to probe the depths. The 65M weighs a full ounce and can be fished as deep as 20 feet with ease, while the larger 85M weighs two ounces. In sardine-style baits, the 43MR is designed to be fished as deep as 10 feet, and the 1 3/8 ounce 53MR down to 20 feet. Very patient fishing can send these lures even deeper--sinking MirrOlures have been used to hook big tarpon at depths of more than 40 feet, though it takes careful line and boat control to get the lures that deep in a flowing tide. The 43 and 53 also function as crankbaits when reeled rapidly--they swim with a tight wobble, and have a bead-filled sound-chamber inside to add a fish-attracting rattle.

DIVING PLUGS

One way to get a piece of buoyant plastic to run deep is to add a diving lip, so MirrOlure offers a full line of divers, many of them suitable for trolling. The jointed 15M and 25M are both snook killers, even though more anglers buy them to fish for bass than snook. The 96MR and 4 7/8" 98MR are both floater/divers that float at rest, dive on retrieve, so they're a good bet where a shallow edge falls off to a deep channel. The 3 1/2" 92MR Shad Rattler

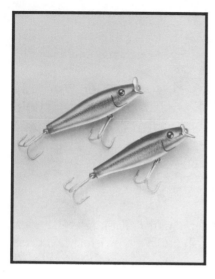

The 88MR is a floating popper with an invertible clear plastic lip. With the small side of the lip down, the plug chugs along on the surface. Turn the lip over to put the large side down and it becomes a wobbler that runs just under the surface like an injured minnow.

readily probes channels down to 10 feet deep due to a larger diving lip. Mark Bennett likes these divers for winter fishing. "Crank them down so they kick up the mud in the residential channels," he suggests. "The fish are down there when it's cold, and these lures can help you sort through a lot of water fast."

For those after lunker snook, the larger divers may be the ticket. The 103 MR is 7 inches long, a great bait for twitching along the mangrove edges. The 107MR runs down to 12 feet when trolled, while the 111MR can be pushed below 20 feet. (All the lipped models are individually tank-tested and tuned to run straight at the factory before shipping--they're ready to fish right out of the box.

COLORS

All of these artificials work well in either silver or gold finish, with black, blue or green backs. They probably would work well in bright pink and orange, too, but it makes sense to "match the hatch" when you can. I have yet to see any pink or orange sardines except the canned ones packed in tomato sauce, but snook sometimes go for variety on the menu.

It's very true that some color patterns you never see in nature catch plenty of fish--a white body with a red head has been a favorite with thousands of snookers for decades. (It's a particular favorite when weather conditions are bad.) That aside, it's usually best to go with lures that resemble the local baitfish, with gold-flash sides and darker bodies in the backwaters, silver-flash and lighter bodies along the beaches.

MirrOlure uses a color-numbering system to designate the patterns, thus a 52M11 is the classic 52 with a red head and white body, while the 52M18 is the same lure body with a green back and white belly.

All MirrOlures have silver or gold inserts inside the lure so that the fish-attracting flash remains visible for the life of the plug. The strong but clear plastic body lets the shine show through.

OTHER LURES

There are dozens of other good lures made by MirrOlure competitors, and it's not a bad idea to carry a few of each type for days when things are slow and you might want to experiment. The soft plastics have proven particularly effective in recent years; imitation shrimp and mullet and the darting worm-like surface lures should be in your box. The latter are completely weedfree when Texas-rigged, and work great around oyster bars and in needle-rush grass.

An assortment of plastic-tail and bucktail jigs in sizes from 1/4 to 1 ounce also belongs aboard. Jigs are unbeatable when the fish are in deep or fast water. Look for jigs with substantial hooks, even in the smaller headweights--some 1/4 ounce jigs have light wire hooks that are fine for trout but bend easily when a big snook heads for the mangroves.

Spoons are not widely recognized as snook lures anymore, but they were a favorite of old-time snookers and they still work. They're particularly effective when "skipped" with a sidearm cast back under the mangroves where conventional lures won't go.

It never hurts to try something new on snook, even though the tried-and-true classics are usually the best bets. Every great new snook lure had to start somewhere--remember that the Sluggo was originally thought of as strictly a bass lure, but now everybody knows it's a killer snook lure, as well as great for trout, reds and tarpon. Tomorrow's classic might be a spinnerbait or a plastic worm; experiment when the pace becomes boring.

TACKLE FOR LURES

All topwaters are best fished on light baitcasting gear with line testing 12 to 14 pounds. You can fish topwaters on spinning gear, but spinning tackle adequate to handle 14-pound-test line is nearly always heavier than a baitcaster of comparable abilities. When you're powering out hundreds of casts over a day, a few ounces makes a big difference.

Heavy line won't work on a small-diameter spinning reel, but it works fine on most revolving spool reels. And since most snook plugs are 1/2 ounce and up, there's plenty of weight to allow the baitcaster to do its thing.

A leader of 20- to 30-pound test mono is necessary to prevent cutoffs on sharp gill covers or barnacle-encrusted pilings and docks. In reality, for big fish you need 40, but that's too heavy for topwater fishing because it interferes with lure action and is highly visible.

Best length is about 12 to 18 inches, and it's wise to use a line-to-line knot -- a double Uni or blood knot -- rather than a swivel, which catches in the rod guides. Tie on the lure with a loop knot so that it can swivel freely for lots of action.

THE TEASE

Success with topwaters depends entirely on getting down what might be called "the tease", a scintillating dance that makes the lure flash, turn, dart and squirm without moving through the water very much at all. It looks a lot like a seriously wounded baitfish trying to escape, and it drives snook bonkers.

The trick is to use the rod, rather than the reel, to move the lure. Captain Jerry Williams of Tampa, a 7M fan, likes to start the action with a sharp snatch of the rod just as the lure hits the water. This makes it "chirp" or splash rather than simply plunking down, and many times that single motion draws a strike. Watch a live baitfish after a leap -- often they scoot along the surface when they fall back. Williams' tactic mimics that motion.

For the retrieve, the rod tip is held low to the water, then snatched toward the boat with a sharp flick of the wrist. The instant the flick is completed, the tip is allowed to drift back toward the lure, creating slack. Only then do you take up the slack with the reel and repeat the twitch.

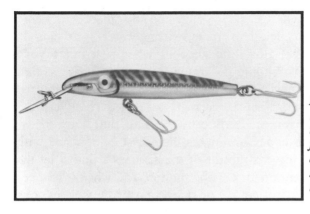

Larger divers like the 112MR are excellent trolling plugs for fishing deep passes and bridges. Big snook seem to like the big mouthful.

This technique causes the lure to splash and flash and dart sideways, but not to move forward much at all. The progression is 6 to 12 inches per twitch, which gives the fish plenty of time to look it over before attacking. Keep it dancing. You don't want "retrievus interruptus" here, the long hesitations you might use for trout or largemouth bass. If a lure stops, a snook forgets about it instantly. But it's not necessary to hurry it back to the boat.

This is not to say a fast retrieve isn't called for at times. In spring, when the fish first hit the flats and are very hungry, they'll sometimes go crazy over a retrieve that moves the lure very briskly. If you see fish looking over your lures but not hitting, try speeding up the retrieve.

One tip offered by expert snooker Eric Bachnik of MirrOlure: if your lure keeps getting the trebles flipped over the leader, you're jerking the lure too hard. Make the twitches shorter, and the problem goes away. Bill LeMaster, company chief, notes that you can avoid tangles on the cast by stopping or slowing the lure just before it hits the water. "The tension on the line brings the eye around toward the boat, puts the hooks under the lure so that they don't catch the leader, and gives a gentler splash," LeMaster advises.

GO WITH THE FLOW

The other secret of catching snook on many lures is to look for strong current. Snook use the current to advantage in feeding more than any other flats species. They home in on creek mouths, bay entries, causeway openings, island points and any other areas where tidal flows are strong enough to create swirling water.   Of course, you have to take that flow into account when you make your presentation. The cast should go uptide, or quartering it, so that your plug drifts back with the flow as you tease it along. Injured minnows don't swim against the current, and snook know it.

One of the great pluses of topwaters is that they allow presentations to fish under overhangs that can't be reached with other lures. You simply cast uptide of the mangrove limbs, let the current carry your bait under the obstruction, and when it reaches the danger zone, give it a couple of sharp pops. Many times, this draws an amazing explosion. Slow sinkers also work for this, provided there are no underwater snags in the spot.

WHEN TO STRIKE

The final problem in lure fishing, particularly with topwaters, is knowing when to set the hook. Snook tend to scare the bejeesus out of you when they hit, and the usual reaction of first-timers is either to 1.- turn to stone and stare, wide-eyed, at the diminishing tidal wave where the snook used to be, or 2.- rear back in panic and send the snookless plug buzzing at mach II toward their partner's head.

Neither puts linesider filets on the table.

Until you have a few hundred topwater strikes behind you and instinctively sense whether or not the fish has the plug, the best approach is to watch the lure closely at all times. Don't look up at the seagulls, down at the minnows or over to the beach at the yellow bikini--watch the plug.

By the time you hear the splash it's too late, so keep your eye directly on the lure. Sometimes you'll actually see the fish's jaws come out of the water and pull down the plug, and that's the time to snatch home the barbs. Other times, there's a big splash but the lure is still there--hold on, give it a few short twitches, and it's likely to disappear. With subsurface lures, the time to strike is usually right now, as soon as you feel the hit--though with soft plastics, you sometimes do better by waiting a second or two for the fish to get the bait deep in its mouth.

With subsurface lures, the time to strike is usually right now, as soon as you feel the hit.

Secondly, remember that you're not tuna fishing with a Calcutta pole. All you have to do is wrist-flick the rod tip a bit to set the hook. And a short strike won't jerk the lure into the next county if you miss the fish. If you make a short, sharp set that misses, the lure will jump forward only a foot or so. When you get control of the line, give it a few quick, sharp twitches. The snook is probably still right there, and very often he comes right back. Maybe he's irritated, maybe hungry, but be ready for that second time around. Once he's got it solidly and starts to run, you can give a second quick hookset for good measure.

If you don't get hit again on that cast, cast immediately to the same spot. Very often the same fish or one hanging with him will strike a second time, and even a third. I had a fish at Charlotte Harbor come up on a topwater seven times—and I never did catch him!   Of course, topwaters are great fish-locators, too. Sometimes the fish roll on a floater but refuse it. Go back to that spot with a swimmer-tail jig or a slow-sinking plug like the 52-M and it's instant hook-up. Keep a couple of rods rigged with sinking lures when you go topwater fishing and be ready to switch quickly when the need arises.

FINE-TUNING YOUR LURES

Most plugs work great right out of the box, but after they've been walloped a few dozen times by big snook they may begin to get a bit gimpy. That's the time to put things back shipshape so that the lure keeps catching fish.

Of course, all experienced anglers soon learn about bending the eye of any lure to get it to run straight. And regular checks of any used lures for bent hooks, lips or propeller blades will keep these baits performing as they should.

Sometimes, even getting one treble out of line when you unhook a fish can take away that special something that makes them love the action. Watch out, too, for pinholes through paint or plastic - a water-logged lure will never perform as it should. Try not to bounce your lures off seawalls, pilings or other hard objects; not even the best of them will stand this treatment long.

It's also smart to rinse your lures in fresh water before putting them away after a trip--even though most saltwater models have corrosion-resistant hooks, they'll last a lot longer if you get rid of the brine.

Lures last a long time, they never die in the bait well and they don't stink when they get old. And, they're a whole lot better investment than shrimp in the long run. But they do need a bit of TLC now and then to keep them performing.

CHAPTER 11

MASTERING LIVE BAITS

There was a time when scaled sardines were a closely guarded secret by Florida's top guides and commercial hook-and-liners. Naturally enough, the pros were not eager to share the reasons for their success.

But the secret is out, and the truth is that there is no other live bait that works half as well as a shimmering, silver-sided sardine free-lined over a snook hole.

Aware of this, in the last three to five years anglers by the thousands have bought cast nets and rigged up live wells to handle these magic baits. The only problem is, there are a limited number of areas where sardines are easy to find.

While sardines are prolific and very fast-growing, producing a fishing-size crop yearly, the areas where anglers can find and catch them best, over grassy shallows covered with clear water, are limited. And some seem to be reaching their limits in terms of castnetting pressure.

"It's harder to catch the bait than the snook some days," says Captain Rob McCue of New Port Richey, who specializes in trophy snook 15 pounds and up. "You have to run 10 miles out and back to get your sardines, and sometimes your fish are just a mile from the dock. You spend two hours catching bait, and then you have your limit of snook in 45 minutes."

One of the problems professional fishermen face is that they need a large number of baitfish to produce hot fishing action. The

Scaled sardines (top) and threadfins are both ideal live baits. The sardines can be chummed into castnet range, but threads or "greenies" don't come to the scent and have to be stalked. The sardines usually survive better in the baitwell.

sardines are used not only on the hook, but also as live chum. Some expert anglers use three times more sardines as chum than as bait.

Scott Moore, the famed Cortez guide whose snook catches run as high as 5,000 per year, figures he needs at least 300 baits to go fishing. Because Moore has been fishing the baits for over 20 years, he knows where to look for them through most of the year, but even he has occasional problems finding them these days in his favorite waters around Charlotte Harbor.

"You used to not see a castnet on one boat in a hundred," says Moore. "These days, just about every boat on the flats has somebody on the platform tossing a net in the morning."

What all of this means is that it now takes more expertise to find and catch sardines than ever before.

LOCATING THE BAITFISH

"The first problem is finding an area where there are baits and not a lot of other boats," says Rob McCue. "If you get a lot of people working on the sardines, they not only thin them out, but the ones that are still around are boat shy. That's why I don't go to the same places where other boats go to get my bait."

The places where most fishermen find their baits are natural sardine attractors. The baitfish like to roam the inner edges of open water, and often move in from these areas to the first turtle grass flat at the edge of deep water.

They're commonly found on the first grassy area inside a pass, and the larger ones often hang around channel markers and range markers in water 8 to 15 feet deep. Rock piles in water 3 to 10 feet deep also sometimes hold pods of sardines, as do piers and other structures that give them some protection from predators.

There are also plenty of scaled sardines in the larger open bays and in the Gulf itself, but finding these fish is a problem since the points of concentration change continuously. Catching them in the deeper water is difficult because successful castnetting usually depends on trapping the fish against bottom. And, the rougher waters offshore often put these baits out of reach for the small, low-freeboard flats boats.

The trick, says McCue, is to find inshore areas that other anglers overlook. Sometimes a scattering of rocks miles from any landmark can be a honeyhole. A fallen marker, a boat wreck or any sort of debris can also be keys to finding them.

"It takes a lot of running and looking, but once you have two or three of these spots, it's money in the bank so long as nobody else finds them."

McCue said that ballyhoo, slender, beaked baitfish that often swim at the surface, are frequently markers for sardines. They hang in the same areas and are much easier to see from a moving boat than the other baitfish.

FATAL ATTRACTION

Once you sight bait—usually by noting their flashing forms and the ripple they make at the surface as they feed—bringing them into castnet range is the next job.

While unmolested bait usually comes quickly to the slightest hint of a chum made from whole wheat bread and canned sardines, the baits are much harder to lure in areas where they are netted frequently.

McCue likes to set up well uptide of whatever structure is holding the baits and lure them to him with chum, rather than anchoring right on the spot and possibly pushing the baits off.

His chum starts with the standard bread/sardine mix, but he adds a major helping of menhaden oil as well. The pungent brown oil is available at baitshops that cater to offshore fishermen.

"The oil makes a slick that spreads out for hundreds of yards," says McCue. "It really seems to have a special appeal for sardines. They'll come to it when they completely ignore the standard chum."

Some anglers, including Scott Moore, also like to add anise oil to the chum mix. Moore also adds canned jack mackerel.

Whatever the mixture, it's dribbled overboard in dime-sized droplets, just enough to create a scent trail that will bring the bait within castnet range, about 10 feet from the boat.

When there are plenty of baits in close, McCue tosses out a "bomb" of chum, a whole handful, which immediately sends the baitfish into a tight swarm as they attack the food. Then it's time to toss the net.

NET RESULTS

Most castnet pros like a net with a nominal measure of 10 to 12 feet. These nets open to a circle about double their nominal size, so cover a lot of water.

"You have to have a big net and one with lots of belly and lots of lead," says McCue. "A flat net, one that's built with a minimum of webbing to keep down cost, won't open right and won't settle over the baits the way it should."

He says that the lead weights on the net should total 15 pounds or more so that they quickly pull the net to bottom, keeping the sardines from swimming out underneath.

His other advice is to make the first throw count.

"You always catch the most on the first throw because they're not spooked then. If you make a bad throw, you're going to miss your best chance."

LIVELY LIVEWELLS

Finally, because bait is getting hard to come by, it also makes sense to equip your boat with a livewell that will keep what you're able to catch healthy all day long. That means a rounded well that holds at least 30 gallons, with a powerful pump supplying a continuous flow of fresh sea water. Many expert sardine fishermen like Capt. James Wisner add a bubbler or aerator to put additional oxygen in the water, as well.

"The idea is not just to keep them alive, but to keep them lively," says McCue. "A bait that really takes off when it hits the water will draw three times as many strikes as one that can barely swim. It pays to do whatever you can to have really frisky bait."

A large castnet with a 10 to 12 foot radius and about 15 pounds of lead is needed for effectively capturing sardines and greenbacks..

THE GLASS MENAGERIE

The annual glass minnow invasion of coastal rivers brings a snook feed completely out of proportion to the minute size of these tiny baits. The minnows, actually juvenile bay anchovies, are only an inch long, but they come into the rivers in countless millions, filling the water from shore to shore with black, swarming masses.

This sort of food supply never goes unnoticed in Nature, and the fish follow. Though it's hard to imagine that large fish would pay much attention to bait that is hardly bigger than a thumbtack, most inshore gamefish stuff themselves with the minnows for as long as they are available. (Remember, the great whales eat krill

Captain Scott Moore likes a mix of jack mackerel, canned sardines, whole wheat bread and anise oil to lure sardines into range. Some anglers also use menhaden oil in the mix.

that are hardly big enough to see with the naked eye—but they eat them by the trainload!)

Even whopper snook can be seen charging through the schools of tiny baits, often with their backs out of water as they crash and churn the surface. The little guys absolutely love them.

Fishing can be ridiculously easy if you get on the areas where the minnows are most dense. Any small silver jig, spoon or ultra-light plug will get hit as it passes among the minnows, and sometimes you may stick several fish on the same cast if the hook comes loose from the first victim.

Among the most effective jigs is an eighth-ounce head rigged with a small silver flake Mann's shad tail. The Cotee shad in silver flake or gold is also effective, as are the smaller Bubba's. A new mini-jig from Mr. Wiffle, which has a large, stout hook but a small head and plastic swimmer body, is also a very good choice. The smallest MirrOlure, the 1 5/8"MM version, also draws strikes.

If you're getting lots of follows but no solid strikes, try shaving down your jig. Usually, lures that are refused are too big. You may have to split the plastic tail in half lengthwise and then take a bit off the head or tail as well, until it gets down near the size of the minnows. It's sometimes necessary to shave a little off the lead as well, since a lighter jig has a slower, more lifelike fall.

The lure is fished on an 18-inch shock leader of 20-pound-test to prevent cutoffs by snook gill plates and the rough mouths of ladyfish. A soft spinning rod and 6- to 8-pound-test mono make it easy to toss the light weight. In clear water, you may have to go to 15-pound-test leader.

If you get the lure in front of the fish, they'll do the rest, often hitting it on the drop. However, finding the right spot to drop it sometimes takes some study. The glass minnows seem to gather in certain areas in great numbers, and are completely absent in others. If you fish where the minnows are missing, you won't catch much, because every fish in the area is likely to be homed in on the baitfish when they're available. They appear to be most abundant in April through June, and again in October and November inshore.

The most obvious way to spot the bait, of course, is to luck up on a feeding frenzy—snook, ladyfish, jacks and trout all busting bait on top. This is most likely to happen on the first part of the rising tide, especially if this happens to come at dawn or dusk.

If you're not lucky enough to see a school of fish breaking, sometimes the concentrations are given away by a few scattered splashes, particularly on flats adjacent to deeper pools where they'll push the bait to attack.

Concentrations of diving pelicans are also a good indicator of minnows in the river. There's not much else to draw pelicans inland, so when you see them crashing well upstream, you can bet the glass minnows are there.

Wading birds also work hard on the minnows, so you might fish in areas where you see a number of egrets or herons busily pecking and gulping.

Finding the minnow aggregations is easiest around dawn on calm mornings, when they come to the surface to feed. It looks like raindrops falling on the water, but the splashes are separated, not all in a wave as they are with threadfins.

Jim Ellington of Ruskin does well by hanging a small jig about 18 inches behind a floating plug from which the hooks have been removed. The plug makes enough noise to attract the fish, and when they see the jig below, they grab it. The Float-n-Jig from Love Lures works on the same principle, but is small enough to cast with spinning tackle. It's a 2-inch slip cork with a 1/8 ounce jig below. For baitcasters, try a larger float like the Flats Equalizer.

Flyrod minnow imitations are super when the fish are on glass minnows, too. Epoxy flies are nearest to the real thing in appearance, but often a simple mono wrap on the shaft with a few strands of bucktail as a tail, ala the Carl Hansen Glass Minnow, will do the job. See the chapter on fly fishing for more details. (You can fish these flies on spinning tackle by adding a cork or a bit of split shot for casting weight.)

The minnows also move into the passes during the early part of the summer spawn, and make up a major food source for the spawning snook. Glass minnow fishing remains good at least through the first cold front most years.

GREENIES

Scaled sardines are the favorite of snookers, but to the snook, other baitfish are just as appealing. Thread herring or "greenbacks" can save a trip when whitebait is tough to locate.

"Threads are more abundant than sardines, and you can always find plenty of them around the bridges and offshore markers," says Capt. John Griffith of Tampa.

Thread herring don't come to chum like sardines, and this can sometimes make them more difficult to spot.

"You may have to use a depthfinder and just throw on the area where they're marking, because you won't be able to pull them up to the back of the boat in shallow water like you can with sardines," says Griffith. "But if you look a while, you'll find a lot of areas where there are always greenbacks as long as the water is reasonably warm."

In general, greenbacks tend to be fish of deeper, open water, while sardines are most often seen on the outer edges of the grass flats. And, while sardines actively attack individual microscopic animals, threads feed mostly by filter-feeding, simply swimming through the planktonic soup of the sea and taking what drifts into their mouths.

The greenbacks, not surprisingly, have dark green or gray backs with silver sides. The "threadfin" designation comes because of a

Glass minnows are tiny, but their attraction for gamefish is huge. They're too small to be used as live bait, but small lures and flies that imitate them can be very effective when fished around bait schools.

threadlike whip on the dorsal fin. The species is actually the thread herring, as distinguished from a much less abundant bottom species, the true threadfin. Thread herring also have a spot behind the gill plate, and their eyes are very small.

Scaled sardines have a silvery body and light tan, almost white backs. They have no thread, no spots and their eyes are much larger than the thread herrings, but otherwise the body shape is very similar.

Scaled sardines survive better in a baitwell than do the greenbacks, but if you don't mind catching bait every three hours or so, the threads will be just as lively.

One of the advantages of threads in the spring is that there are usually plenty of big ones around. The big snook really prefer a 4- to 5-inch bait, and sardines that size are rare until late summer or fall.

Greenies, like sardines, are usually fished unweighted, on size 1/0 or 2/0 short-shank hooks that allow them to swim freely. The hook is placed either through the nose or at the joint of the pectoral fin. About 18 inches of 30-pound-test mono is used as shock leader.

SHRIMP

It's an amateur's bait.

That's the attitude of many experienced saltwater anglers about shrimp, which is the bait of choice for the multitudes of casual fishermen who soak these crustaceans from bridges, piers, shorelines and rented rowboats.

Fished in the typical fashion by the "duffers" of the fishing world, shrimp are, indeed, not very effective. Impaled on a 6/0 hook and weighted down with a 3-ounce egg sinker, they're something less than irresistible to snook and other gamefish.

But particularly in winter, shrimp come into their own as live baits. Fished with a bit of finesse and in the right locations, they can produce very well, and are even a match for the scaled sardine much revered by live-bait experts. In fact, one mark of the master snook fishermen is his ability to use live shrimp as the deadly bait it is.

One caveat—some conservationists report that bait-shrimping results in a considerable by-catch of juvenile fish, many of which don't survive being released as they are culled from the live shrimp. Bait-shrimping reportedly does not generate the waste that food-shrimping does in some areas, but it can be a factor in overall fish populations where it's practiced heavily, as along the grass flats from Anclote Key northward. For that reason, some anglers refuse to fish live shrimp. But there's no denying its success. Follow your conscience on this one.

Fishing shrimp effectively starts with selecting top-quality baits, and with keeping them lively. Most bait shop owners will, for a slight added charge per dozen, pick out "select" or slightly larger shrimp. For those who want to catch larger snook or jumbo trout and reds, these baits have a particular appeal.

Using light gear is the real key to success with shrimp. Top fishermen use it in the same way as live sardines, fished completely unweighted, on light-wire 1/0 bait hooks, slipped sideways under the horn or crest on the head. Hooked this way, and fished on 6- to 8-pound test on a light spinning rig, shrimp can be cast good distances and will swim naturally. Heavier, larger hooks don't work with shrimp—they can't handle the weight.

A second method, used when longer casts are called for, is to clip off the tail fin so the bait won't spin, and run the hook through the first joint of the tail. This is a more durable hook-up than the crest hook-up, allowing you to apply more force to the cast, though the bait doesn't swim as naturally once it gets there.

The best shrimp anglers fish these delicate baits much as they would an artificial, tossing them around mangroves, near barnacled pilings and rock piles, and allowing them to flutter down into deep holes in residential canals and around the hot-water outflows of area powerplants. (A bit of weight is added in water deeper than 5 feet.)

The baits are moved continuously. If allowed to settle into one spot, they'll soon fall victim to catfish or pinfish, so keeping them up and swimming is the best program. It also makes them more noticeable to snook and other gamefish.

The baits are cast uptide, allowed to sweep down with the flow past a likely area, and then retrieved for another cast. This naturally goes through a lot of shrimp, but it also catches a lot of fish. Most experts use a shrimp for five or six throws, then discard it into the chum bucket and get a fresh one.

Shrimp have the ability to act as "fish-finders" at times, for those alert enough to notice. When a fish approaches a shrimp underwater, the bait usually makes a quick dart that can be felt in the rod tip. When a snook comes up from underneath, the bait dashes to the surface and sometimes take off in a series of jumps, dragging the line behind it.

If you note any of these warning signs, it means a fish was tempted. Keep a close eye on the bait and be ready for action. If you don't get bit, reel in, rebait and put a fresh bait back in the same spot, then hang on.

Shrimp are also effective in locating fish scattered in larger canals and waterways. They can be slow-trolled in a Pico "shrimp harness", which keeps them upright and prevents spinning. Fished this way, the baits can cover a lot of water, and any fish they pass will be alerted by both the form and the scent.

They can also be fished under a popping cork or Mansfield Mauler, a particularly deadly technique for drifting baits to snook when they're found under dock lights at night, as they so often are throughout the west coast of Florida in winter. A sharp pull on the line brings a "baloop!" sound from the cork that is much like a snook hitting a shrimp on top. Any linesiders within hearing quickly home in on the noise.

If you can't quite bring yourself to fish shrimp whole due to the prices, they make great "tipping" bait, cut into 1/2 inch pieces and put on the hooks of a jig. The added scent will draw hits from all fish that love shrimp—which includes just about all species in saltwater.

Shrimp also make excellent, if somewhat expensive, live chum. You can often get a hundred small shrimp for around $7 or $8, and if you toss four or five of these out to drift down a mangrove shoreline, they'll act as fish-finders the same way that live sardines do. The "free" baits turn on the fish and bring them to the top. When you deliver one with a hook attached the action is usually immediate.

Finally, if you try all this and don't catch any fish, you can always eat the bait. Boiled, with a little Cajun sauce, if you please.

CHAPTER 12

FLY-RODDING FOR SNOOK

Catching a 30-pound snook on any tackle is a feat worth remembrance. Catching one on a flyrod is an angling achievement that many thought would never happen. But it did happen, a few years ago in Everglades National Park.

Fishing out of Chokoloskee, about 30 miles east of Naples, Captain Pete Villani and his angler, Dr. Rex Garrett of Sarina, Ontario, were poling down a murky tidal creek just after sunup when Villani spotted the tell-tale yellow dorsal and tail of a snook finning along at the surface.

"It had been unusually cold for April," Villani said. "The sun was shining on the shallow mud flats, and I think the fish was in there trying to warm up."

Garrett, an experienced fly-caster but a novice to snook fishing, presented a red and white deer hair MirrOlure Fly, a slider with weighted eyes, on 8-weight tackle.

"The fish ignored the first three casts," said Villani. "It sank out of sight on the third toss, and I thought that was it. But in a little while, it popped back up."

Garrett placed the fly just right on the fourth toss, and the fish took immediately. It was only after the battle went beyond 10 minutes that Villani realized how big the linesider really was. It scaled 30 pounds, 4 ounces—a new all-tippet record in the International Game Fish Association flyfishing division. The fish was 43 inches long and had a girth of 25 1/2 inches.

The snook was taken on 20-pound class tippet, and holds that record as well as the all-tippet record. It displaced a 27.5 pound fish taken at St. Lucie Inlet that same spring.

FLY TACKLE AND TACTICS

It's not likely that you'll get a 30-pounder on fly tackle, but snook readily take a variety of flyrod lures. While the record fish was taken on 8-weight tackle, many snook experts prefer 10 weight rods for mangrove country fishing because the added power gives some chance of stopping a fish from getting to the roots and cutting your leader. And, because the casts are often short and with little room for a backcast, overloading the rods with weight-forward 12-weight line is common. The heavier line makes it easier to flex the rod and make a good cast with a short length out the tip.

TAKE US TO YOUR LEADER

Leaders? Forget the light stuff unless you're specifically after an IGFA tippet class. For snook, 16-pound is light enough to get the hits, and that's as light as you ought to go both for the sake of your won/loss record and for the sake of the fish. Otherwise, you'll leave a lot of snook with your flies stuck in their mouths for weeks. The exception is when you find fish out on the flats or in the open passes with no hidey-hole nearby where they can cut you off. Lighter leaders can do the job in these areas.

You need a foot of shock leader after the lightest tippet section, of course—30-pound test is usually best, but you may have to go to 25 or even 20 in extremely clear water like that found on the west coast flats at times.

Mason's Hard Mono is the recognized standard for building leaders, with the right amount of stiffness for turning over big flies and good abrasion resistance. Capt. Bill Miller of Tampa boils his leader sections for a few minutes in long, straight pans to remove the curl, and this is a good idea particularly for the heavier butt sections. Some anglers have gone to the fluorocarbon leaders of late because they're less visible. The material is very expensive, but it does seem to be pretty much invisible below the surface.

A typical snook leader would be 8 to 9 feet long, starting with 4 feet of 30, blood-knotted or double-uni-knotted to a couple feet of 20, knotted to the lightest tippet section, 16 or 12 or whatever,

Snook are not easy to catch on flies by day, but when you make a hookup the spectacular fight makes it worth the wait. Most anglers use 8-weight gear on the flats, 10-weight around the mangroves.

and finished off with the shock leader. If you're interested in someday entering a fish as an IGFA flyrod record, make your tippet section no less than 15 inches long, and your shock leader no more than 12 inches long, including all the knots. The shock leader might best be tied on with an Albright, which handles the different diameters better than a Uni or blood knot. (If you hate to tie knots, you can do pretty well with a two-segment leader, a 30-pound-test butt and then straight 20 all the way to the fly.)

I prefer to tie flies to the shock with a loop knot, usually a seven-times-around Uni, drawing down the loop until it's just slightly bigger than the eye of the hook. You don't want a big loop because it catches moss, but you don't want it so small that it binds and cuts down the action of the fly, either.

Some very good anglers prefer to snell their snook flies, with the shock leader built right in, and they catch plenty with that arrangement, too—it comes through the water more cleanly, which can be an advantage when there's a lot of loose moss.

Whopper snook like this one, taken by angler Rick Cannon while being guided by Captain Phil Chapman, are lifetime catches on the fly. This fish was captured from a pothole in Charlotte Harbor.

BEST FLIES

Nearly any fly two to five inches long can be used for snook, but some of the best patterns include the venerable Lefty's Deceiver, the Seaducer, the Glass Minnow, Clouser Minnow, epoxy shrimp, Krystal Shrimp, Black Leech and a variety of floating, soft foam sliders and poppers. Sizes are usually 1/0 to 2/0.

It's my experience you catch more fish on the slow-sinking flies, but it's a lot more fun to get that amazing surface strike on the poppers.

Of course, all flies work a lot better after you chunk over three or four live sardines to get the fish in a feeding mood. A few "free" shrimp drifted under a dock or down a mangrove edge can have the same effect — chumming definitely helps.

WHEN TO FLY FISH

Best times for fly-rodding? When the glass minnow run is in full swing on either coast is prime. The fish are homed in on fly-rod sized baits, and if you can get your offering to them, they're highly likely to inhale it. The glass minnows, incidentally, move a lot slower than some of the other critters a snook pursues—the retrieve motion is more short twitches than the big strips you might use for other saltwater flies.

There are some glass minnows or bay anchovies around much of the year, but the fishing action is usually best in spring and through June, when fish stacked up in the passes have to home in on whatever is close to the spawning aggregations. There's another surge of the tiny minnows in October most years.

DOCK FISH

One killer approach for fly-rodders is to fish a shrimp pattern around dock lights after sundown. While dock fish are notoriously suspicious about artificials, they often gobble up tiny fly-rod offerings without a second thought. Most of the fish you'll catch this way will be on the short side of 24 inches, but you'll get lots of them, and the fights tend to be frantic as you try to keep them away from the pilings.

Fishing the docks with flies requires the same sort of approach as with live bait or plugs—anchor at the edge of casting range, keep quiet, deliver the fly uptide of the fish and let the current bring it to them as you activate it.

I generally work on the outer edges of the light first because some large fish sometimes hold in the shadows. If that doesn't do the job, deliver to the little guys floating directly below the light. A cast that drops just under the dock and then swims out nearly always gets nailed.

Remember, when you catch a fish out of a confined area like this, the disturbance of the fight often puts the other fish down, but they won't stay down long if you sit quietly. Put your rod aside and drink a cup of coffee, and the fish will usually rise back to their feeding positions in a few minutes.

PASS ACTION

Some big snook are caught in the passes during summer on flies. In fact, most of the IGFA tippet-class records have been caught in these areas from June through August during the closed season. There are two likely reasons—first, the fish are concentrated in large, observable schools which cuts down on the blind casting,

Overhanging mangroves are ideal fly-rod country. However, it takes a powerful rod to pull the fish away from the cover once they're hooked.

and second, there's less pressure on them than during the open season.

Phil Chapman, biologist with the Florida Game and Fresh Water Fish Commission, used a fly rod, sinking line and a selection of black streamers at Marco Pass to collect dozens of big snook for the state's first effort at artificially-induced spawning in snook in the late 1970's. Chapman said that after dark, the snook grabbed the flies readily, and there was less damage to the fish than there might have been with live bait.

Fishing the passes is a matter of letting the tide do the fishing for you, much like fishing in a fresh water trout stream. You cast as

Shrimp imitations like this one can be effective around lighted docks after dark. Flies are sometimes the most effective of all lures around these docks, though the average size of the fish they catch tends to be smaller than with larger lures.

far uptide as possible and then try to take up the belly of line that forms as the tide brings the lure down to you.

Too much belly will cause the fly to run faster than the water and rise to the surface. Sinking lines are required for this work, and some who practice it regularly wrap their flies in copper wire to keep them down.

MANGROVE COUNTRY

If you fish the Everglades creeks in winter—a very good choice for flyrodders—you'll need to learn both the roll cast and the steeple cast to avoid the mangroves that block backcasts just about everywhere. The roll is well-known, keeping the line in front of you as you deliver short casts to a series of holes along the shoreline.

The steeple is a redirection of the backcast upward rather than aft, managed basically by shortstroking the backcast and tilting the wrist to send the line upward at about 45 degrees, hopefully clearing the mangroves behind you. It's an easy cast once you visualize what you're trying to do, and it allows more distance than the roll for most anglers.

A few words on fighting fish on the fly: while you can pull any direction you like on fish hooked in open water, keeping them out of nearby mangroves requires the "down-and-dirty" rod action devised by Stu Apte for big tarpon. By lowering the rod tip almost to water level and pulling sideways, you can often turn a fish that's determined to make it to his barnacle-encrusted hideout. Pulling upward on this same fish is likely to have little effect, and may tangle your line in the limbs overhanging the shoreline.

One of the nice things about using a fly in the blackwater creeks is that you don't have to make long casts, and the pre-measured length of the fly line out the tip acts as a nice gauge for repeatedly hitting the shoreline just right, so long as you keep the boat at a constant distance. You can toss a popper into an overhung hole, give it three or four pops covering a yard or so, and then lift it out and drop it another 10 feet down the shore, all without ever turning the reel handle. It's highly efficient fishing and tremendous fun when the fish are "on".

I'm an advocate of doing whatever works, and there are plenty of times when fly fishing doesn't. Hard-pressed fish in clear water are a recipe for frustration and a sore casting arm if you try for them on the fly, and in those conditions I'm likely to break out spinning gear and live sardines. But there are times when fly fishing is as good as and maybe better than any other technique, and there's no question that landing a big linesider on the long rod is an angling achievement. It's worth keeping one in your quiver.

CHAPTER 13

LIFESTYLES OF LINESIDERS

Thanks to fees paid for saltwater licenses and snook stamps by anglers, scientists with Florida's Marine Research Labs in St. Petersburg now know far more about snook populations than they did just a few years ago. The fees support research programs that were not even considered in the days when the only official interest was in commercial species.

Lead researcher Ron Taylor spent five years on the water documenting the life history, seasonal migrations, growth and survival rates of the species. His work and that of other researchers at FMRL has created a data-bank on snook that simply didn't exist a decade ago, and that will prove invaluable in managing the species for decades to come.

According to Taylor, snook stocks are currently in good shape, but the numbers of big fish could be improved by some fine-tuning of regulations.

He believes that the 1989 freeze killed tens of thousands of snook around the state. Since snook are a long-lived species, with some reaching more than 15 years old, that freeze may impact the numbers of larger fish into the next century.

MORE SNOOKERS

But even more important, says Taylor, is the huge increase in snook fishing pressure since about 1990.

"The number of snook fishermen has gone straight up, and even with the two-fish limit, that means a lot of fish are being taken," Taylor said.

Male snook don't grow much after reaching 23 inches in length according to Florida DEP research. Most keeper-sized fish like these are females.

Based on the number of tags sold, there are more than 130,000 anglers who specifically target snook each year. And this does not include the thousands more who make limit catches regularly by fishing with flats guides. The number of guides has also increased geometrically in the last five years.

Based on field interviews, Taylor estimates that anglers now make approximately one million trips for snook on the west coast and about 800,000 trips for snook on the east coast yearly. In 1982, the first year for which Taylor has a reasonably accurate estimate, he believes there were only about 100,000 trips specifically for snook on each coast each year. Thus, the pressure has multiplied by a factor of 8 to 10 while the amount of snook habitat has remained the same.

Based on creel surveys, Taylor says that some 800,000 snook are caught per year throughout the west coast range, roughly from Hudson to the 10,000 Islands, and about 600,000 are caught along the east coast, from Cape Canaveral southward.

SNOOK MORTALITY

He says that only about one in 10 of those fish are kept. The annual harvest on each coast is around 50,000; total kill by fishermen each year somewhere near 100,000 fish.

Based on release mortality studies in which snook were held up to 10 days in net pens, Taylor believes that no more than 10 percent of snook caught and released die, and that it's likely the figure is closer to 3 percent.

"We're pretty much convinced that catch-and-release is a good way to provide a good fishing experience for a lot of anglers without hurting the stocks," Taylor says. "If snook are handled carefully and put back into the water promptly, most survive."

EAST VS WEST

Though the common snook, *Centropomis undecimalis*, is the same species throughout Florida waters, there are slight genetic differences between fish on the east coast and those on the west according to FMRL genetics researcher Mike Tringali.

"You can't see a physical difference in the fish, but if you look at the genes, there are a number of variations," says Tringali. He says the break line seems to be roughly Florida Bay; fish to the west of there have the west coast markers, while those from Biscayne Bay northward have the east coast markers.

Based on tag returns, biologists believe that there is little migration of fish through the Florida Keys from east to west coasts—in fact, only one fish has made the crossing, and that fish, tagged on the east coast near St. Lucie Inlet, showed up on the west coast near the Caloosahatchee River. It may have swam through the canals leading to Lake Okeechobee, where there's a resident population of landlocked snook, then passed on through the lock system to make the journey westward.

East coast snook grow faster and reach larger average sizes than those on the west coast. Whether this is the result of more food availability, less water temperature variation or genetics is not known, but the difference is evident in angler's catches. The typical east coast fish approaches 10.7 pounds and 30 inches, while the average west coast fish is 7.95 pounds and less than 24 inches, according to Taylor.

SNOOK MIGRATIONS

East coast fish are far more migratory than west coast snook, roaming many miles between passes according to tag returns. This may be the result of pursuing the annual mullet migrations along the beaches. The bait travels north in spring, south in fall.

According to DEP researcher Jim Whittington, one snook tagged at Jupiter went to Sebastian Inlet, 60 miles away, in 14 days before recapture. Another went from Jupiter to Ponce De Leon Inlet near Daytona, 142 miles, following the fall run of bait. Similar southward movements were recorded, but few made it to the Florida Keys and none made it into the Gulf of Mexico.

West coast fish tend to remain in the same estuarial system where they are hatched, with Tampa Bay fish rarely traveling to Charlotte Harbor, for example. This may mean that each system should be managed separately, almost like a landlocked lake. They travel east and west, up the rivers in fall, out to the beaches in spring, but not north and south.

SNOOK BIOLOGY

Taylor's research indicates that male east coast snook grow faster than males on the west coast, but female growth is similar on both coasts.

Taylor also noted that west coast snook spawn about a month earlier than east coast fish, beginning in mid-April and continuing through early September. East coast fish begin spawning in June and continue to early October. Presently, the closed season runs from June through August, but this leaves spawners vulnerable in May on the west coast and in September on the east coast.

Taylor says the fish spawn in cycles, with individual fish releasing eggs about every 5 to 7 days throughout the spawning cycle. Most spawning takes place in passes along the beach, in channels flowing from smaller bays and around major points with high current flow. He believes the spawn is primarily in the evening, from 6 p.m. until midnight.

Snook range extends north to about New Port Richey on the west coast of Florida, but there are fishable populations in spring-fed rivers as far north as Crystal River. Captain Eric Coppin shows a nice one from the Weeki Wachee.

The female is pursued by a school of males, which repeatedly bump her with their snouts to encourage release of eggs. A mature female produces a lot of eggs: a 33-incher examined by researchers carried an estimated 1.2 million. While only a fraction of these survive, this fecundity makes it possible for populations to snap back quickly when depleted.

Within three weeks after the hatch, the larvae (they look more like tiny insects than fish at this stage) are carried by the tides to shallow creeks, mangrove shores and mosquito impoundments. They can survive in low-oxygen environments because they can take air directly from the surface, like tarpon, until they reach a length of about 4 inches according to researcher Grant Gilmore.

The young fish grow about 1 mm per day for the first 200 days. At a size of 7 to 8 inches they begin to leave the backwaters and head for the shallow grass flats where they start to feed on glass minnows and small shrimp. By age 2 to 3 and lengths of 15 to 18 inches, nearly all have left the backwaters and moved to the flats.

SEX SWAPPERS

Ron Taylor says that snook are what scientists call "protandric hermaphrodites"—that is, all females begin life as males, but some undergo a sex reversal to become egg-producers. The discovery

Snook can adapt to a wide variety of habitats. Mature fish are abundant in deep shipping basins like this one in downtown Tampa.

was made when researchers collecting fish for studies noted that they never caught any females less than 397 millimeters long (about 16 inches). Conversely, they never collected any males more than 925 millimeters long (about 36 inches).

He said that studies of the gonads of fish in the 12-15 inch range revealed that some fish undergo a sex change, perhaps based on a given population's need for females, at around age two or three.

He noted that male fish slow down in growth when they reach about 23 inches, adding little length yearly after that despite life spans that may extend to 13 years. Females are known to live at least 19 years and achieve lengths of over 50 inches.

In ideal conditions, they grow very rapidly: a fish found dead at the St. Lucie Powerplant a few years ago weighed 33 pounds but was aged at only 9 years old according to the otoliths or ear bones. (Scientists learn the age of fish by sectioning these bones, staining them and then counting the annual growth rings, much as is done with trees.)

SNOOK HATCHERIES

So why can't biologists use the state's saltwater hatchery to boost snook populations? Thus far, snook have proven difficult to rear in the hatchery. The adults are very sensitive to handling, and even when a quantity of eggs are hatched, providing the microscopic live food that the larval snook require has proven impossible thus far.

There's some doubt that stocking is highly successful at increasing wild fish populations in any case due to predation. But Taylor says the research should continue in the event a catastrophic freeze wipes out an entire estuary at some time in the future. (The absolute bottom line for snook survival appears to be a water temperature of about 45 degrees Fahrenheit. While most fish can survive 55 and some fish can handle 50 if the drop is gradual, in lab tests none made it below 7 degrees Centigrade, or about 44.6 degrees F.)

Another caution in stocking is that the varied strains of snook may not be interchangeable. It's possible that East Coast fish might exhibit some trait that wouldn't work well in West Coast habitat, and vice versa. So researchers say they won't make use of a single hatchery strain of fish for statewide stocking—fish from a given estuary would be used for stocking only in that estuary.

Of course, it's possible that shuttling snook from one coast to another could be the best thing that ever happened to anglers. Most bass fishermen are aware of the huge success created by transferring Florida-strain largemouths to California, Texas and other southern states: state records in most of these areas are now held by Florida fish or Florida hybrids. As funding becomes available, it might be a good idea for researchers to look into the possibility of cross-breeding the strains to seek hybrid vigor and creation of a "super-snook" strain. Imports of black snook from the Pacific might be a path to controlled lab experiments with hybrids somewhere down the road, though biologists are always nervous about introducing alien species.

HOPE AT MOTE

Researchers at Mote Marine Labs in Sarasota have now discovered a number of promising live foods, including larval oysters and clams, that are readily accepted by the tiny snook and may offer a way around the feeding problems in hatchery production.

"Juvenile redfish readily take pelletized food and we can put whatever they need into it," says biologist Carole Neidig. "But snook are very picky, and usually insist that most of their food be alive. It's been a bottleneck, but it seems we're going to get past it now."

The researchers at Mote are also studying how well stocked fish survive, and how they fit into wild populations. The program will include electronic tagging of juveniles via injecting micro-chip ID tags into them. These tags can be read with an electronic scanner when a fish is recaptured later, giving data on where and when it was released.

KEEPING UP WITH KEEPERS

Ron Taylor reports that numbers of keeper-sized fish, over 24 inches long, have declined as a percent of the catch on the west coast, dropping from an average of near 20 percent in 1990 to as little as 4 percent in 1995 in studies conducted on Tampa Bay. At Naples, 40 percent of the fish reported were legal in 1986, while by 1994 only 2 percent legal fish were reported. In Tampa Bay, netting stuides show a decline of about 3 inches in the average size of snook over the last five years.

"We know these figures are not exact, and maybe some fishermen, particularly the guides, might be doing better, but it gives us trends to help evaluate the direction the fishery is taking," Taylor says.

CHAPTER 14

THE SNOOK FAMILY TREE

Snook are thought to have evolved from a prehistoric ancestor that took shape in the days when the continents were still part of one massive land mass that paleontologists call Pangera. As the continents drifted apart (they are still drifting, at a few inches a year) the "perciform" fishes on the new continents began to evolve slightly differently to meet the challenges of their changing habitat.

Fast-forward a few million years and here we are with the snooks (*Centrompomidae*) in the Americas, Nile perch (*Lates niloticus*) in Africa and barramundi (*Lates calcarifer*) in northern Australia, southern China and India. They're all classified as being Centrompomid fishes, and if you look at them side by side it's pretty clear they're related but not identical. The most obvious physical differences are that the snooks have a forked tail and a rather streamlined body, while the "Lates" species have rounded tails and fatter bodies. All share the obvious lateral line, the flattened forehead and the elongated snout common to the snook of the Americas.

NILE PERCH

The Nile perch is a completely fresh water species found in the White Nile, the Blue Nile and the lakes and streams that spawn these rivers in Central Africa. It's thought to reach sizes approaching 500 pounds. (Try that baby on your 8-weight fly rod!) The IGFA record is just over 191 pounds as this is written. There's a growing commercial fishery for the species on Lake Victoria, where hundreds of tons are taken each year. Some of that catch is imported to the

U.S. where it's marketed as "Lake Victoria snook". Some anglers wish it wasn't, concerned that snook on the menu may lead to poaching here. In any case, I've tasted them, and while the meat does not have the texture of true snook, it's a very light, delicious fish. A limited sport-fishery exists in Kenya, where anglers troll big diving plugs to connect. Coloration of the Nile perch is brown or olive on the back, silver on the sides.

BARRAMUNDI

The barramundi lives in more classic snook habitat; it grows up in fresh water but moves to the river mouths to spawn in brackish water. There's a substantial sport fishery along the coast of northern Australia. The tactics of any good U.S. snooker would do the job on the thunder from down under. In fact, the 'bara even has knife-edged gill plates just like the snook, requiring anglers to use heavy shock leaders to prevent cut-offs.

They're aggressive surface feeders, often attack from under overhanging branches or around structure, and fight like crazy. And they're big—they regularly exceed 50 pounds and are known to reach sizes of at least 120 pounds! Coloration is similar to the snook, green on the back, silver below.

SNOOK OF THE AMERICAS

The Centropomus strain further evolved in the waters of North, Central and South America to create at least 12 identifiable species of snook or robalo. The man who "wrote the book" on species identification is Dr. Luis Rivas of the University of Miami, with a report published by the American Society of Ichthyologists in 1986.

Rivas used differences in ray and scale counts as well as body shape to distinguish the various species. He recognizes six species in the Atlantic, six in the Pacific—and Rivas writes that eight of these species form "transisthmian pairs", which means that they were once the same fish, but evolved slightly differently when the oceans were divided by the emergence of the Central American plateau. No single species inhabits both oceans, according to Rivas' classification system. Four strains, the common snook, tarpon snook, small-scale fat snook and the sword spine snook are found in U.S. waters.

This Costa Rican beauty (the fish, guys, the fish) tend to be heavier than snook of similar length from Florida. The undecimalis strain has the same genetics in both areas, however. Snook on the Pacific side of Central America look much the same, but are made up of several different strains.

It's likely there are so many species because snook tend to remain in their home estuaries. The lack of opportunity for interbreeding with distinct populations would aid evolution of unique traits that eventually changed the physical characteristics of some populations enough to make them a different species.

The common snook is the mainstay of Florida fishing. It's one of three large snook strains, the others being the white snook and the black snook. Both of the latter are found only in Central and South America.

COMMON SNOOK

The common snook, *Centropomus undecimalis*, is the one that interests most anglers. It has the widest distribution, ranging from Pamlico Sound, North Carolina (rarely) to Rio de Janeiro, Brazil. Common snook are not found in fishable numbers north of Florida's "Snook Line", extending roughly from Chassahowitzka on the west coast to Daytona Beach on the east coast, but occasional wanderers are caught much farther up both coasts; a 16-pounder was taken at the mouth of the Mississippi River a few years ago.

No other species is found so far north, indicating that undecimalis has a greater tolerance for cold weather than other strains. In fact, there has been only one report of any other species north of Florida. Common snook are also found in some number in the southern end of the Laguna Madre of Texas and in some of the deep south Texas ports, though that population plummets anytime there's a severe freeze.

The west coast of Panama holds both white and black snook as well as several other strains. Blacks appear to be the largest of all snooks, with the IGFA record currently at 57 pounds, 12 ounces.

The IGFA all-tackle record, as every snooker knows, is 53 pounds, 10 ounces, taken along the beach at Rio Parismina, Costa Rica by Gil Ponzi on Oct. 18, 1978.

WHITE SNOOK

The white snook, *Centropomus viridis*, is the closest relative of the common snook, but it's found only on the Pacific Coast. Range is throughout Baja and the Gulf of California, along Central America's coastline and south to Paita, Peru. This species is also found at the Galapagos Islands, a curiosity to biologists since there are no freshwater rivers there to allow the young to move into brackish nursery areas thought necessary for survival, and the Galapagos are 650 miles from the mainland. They reach at least 40 pounds—as this is written, the IGFA record is 39 pounds, 8 ounces, from Cabo San Lucas, Mexico. The fishery is in murky mangrove rivers in winter, around the outside passes in summer.

BLACK SNOOK

The other major sport species is the black snook, *Centropomus nigrescens*, another Pacific species. The range overlaps with the white snook, and the two look very similar, but the black has a

129

black or olive back and sides while these areas are light gray or white in the white snook. However, the color can vary depending on habitat—the only dependable way to separate the two is via a count of the dorsal fin rays (nine for whites, 10 for blacks) and a few other subtle differences including a longer anal spine on whites. Blacks appear to be the largest of all snook species, and probably account for the tales of six-footers seen in Mexican fish markets over the years. The IGFA record is 57 pounds, 12 ounces, taken at Quepos, Costa Rica in 1991—thus giving Costa Rica the distinction of having produced the record for both common and black snook.

OTHER SNOOKS

The Mexican snook, *Centropomus poeyi*, reaches lengths of about 35 inches. It's found along the Gulf coast of Mexico south to Porto Alegre, Brazil. It has also been reported from Cuba, Jamaica, Haiti and the Virgin Islands. It looks much like the common snook, and can only be distinguished by counting fin rays, gill rakers and scales.

Tarpon snook, *Centropomus pectinatus*, is found on both coasts of Florida and southward to Bahia, Brazil. It's a small species, never recorded much over 20 inches. Larry Larsen, publisher of this book, currently holds the IGFA record for the species. The tarpon snook record weighed 2 pounds 8 ounces and was caught December 1995 in the Rio San Juan in Nicaragua. The underslung jaw is more prominent than in the common snook, making the face look more similar to a tarpon.

The blackfin snook, *Centropomus medius,* is the Pacific Coast twin of the tarpon snook, and reaches lengths around 18 inches. The current IGFA record of 5 pounds, 8 ounces is held by snook specialist Craig Whitehead, a doctor from Tampa, who caught it in Costa Rica. It's most common in the Gulf of California and southward along the coast of Columbia.

The smallscale fat snook, *Centropomus parallelus*, is caught in Florida with some frequency, though it's much less numerous than the common variety. The fish appears to be rotund, less streamlined than common snook, thus the name. The IGFA record is 7 pounds, 4 ounces, taken near Miami. The range includes both

All the snook strains feed on much the same prey, so minnow imitating lures are always effective. There are four strains of snook in U.S. waters, but only <u>undecimalis</u> attains sizes over 10 pounds.

coasts of Florida, the shores of Mexico and southward into Brazil. Parallelus, more than other snook species, tends to travel far up coastal rivers, and is rarely found in water that has a high salt content.

The species has a very close relative designated the largescale fat snook, *Centropomus mexicanus*, which ranges along the east coast of Mexico and around the rivers of Brazil. As you'd expect, the main distinguishing point is scales larger than the fat snook—body shape is much the same. Mexicanus apparently prefers saltwater to brackish or fresh. Largest reported was about 17 inches.

The swordspine snook, *Centropomus ensiferus*, is a small Atlantic species with a distinctive long, sharp spine on the anal fin. Maximum size is reported as 14 inches, and the range includes Florida's east coast, Cuba, Mexico, Panama, Venezuela and northern Brazil.

The longspine snook, *Centropomus armatus*, looks much like the swordspine, but it's a Pacific species. It has the distinctive long, sharp anal spine. Maximum recorded length is about 15 inches, range from Mazatlan, Mexico to La Tola, Ecuador.

The little snook, *Centropomus robalito*, is apparently well named, with no specimen ever recorded over 13.6 inches long. This species also looks much like the swordspine, but is found only on the Pacific coast, from Sonora, Mexico south to Panama.

The humpback snook, Centropomus unionensis, sports a shoulder hump much like a spawning salmon. It's a Pacific species with the most restricted range of all the snooks, from Union Bay, El Salvador to Tumbes, Peru. Largest known size is about 14 inches.

SNOOKING GRAND SLAM

The distinction among species makes it possible for well-heeled snook fanatics to go for a snook "grand slam", in which they attempt to catch all the species, in the same way wild turkey hunters go after the various species of turkeys. The one angler who has probably come closest is Dr. Craig Whitehead of Tampa, Florida, who has prowled the coasts of Central America for 30 years chasing the various species. You may never have the opportunity to hook them all, but even taking the four species available in Florida is an achievement.

FISHING CENTRAL AMERICA

In general, snook fishing in Central and South America lacks both facilities and guides, making it tough to get at the more exotic species. The exception is the Carribean coast of Costa Rica, which actually has too many snook camps — the fishery has been knocked down by the combined pressure of hundreds of tourist anglers plus commercial hook-and-lining. At times you'll stand shoulder-to-shoulder with other anglers at the river mouths, and the fishing is definitely not what it was a decade ago. However, this is the area that produced the world record common snook, and there are probably others there somewhere.

The best approach is to head for one of the new camps that occasionally open in the remote areas. First guys in usually have spectacular action, though they may have to suffer through bad roads and poor accommodations to get at it. The southeast coast of Nicaragua is apparently very good, and some areas in the Yucatan Peninsula of Mexico have also been turning out big fish. Efforts are underway to establish camps on the Pacific coast. Pan Anglers at (312)263-0328 knows all the ins and outs of the area, as does Trek International, (800)654-9915.

CHAPTER 15

ATLANTIC COAST SNOOKING

Florida's east coast doesn't look like classic snook country. High-rise condos are more common than mangroves, and dredged channels have replaced much of the grass flats. But snook are adaptable, and in fact the east coast from Cocoa Beach southward offers some of the best snook fishing in Florida, and may be the best water anywhere in the world for lunkers today.

SNOOK OF A DIFFERENT STRIPE

The fish are larger than those on the west coast—snook of 10 to 15 pounds are common on the east coast in summer, but have become scarce on the west.

The difference in fishing pressure could also be a factor. Snook are targeted, but they're not considered the creme-de-la-creme with sailfish, dolphin and wahoo just three miles offshore. Thus, they don't get the year-around pressure of west coast snook, and more of them survive to old age.

The snook of the east coast are a slightly different strain than west coast fish. They're not different enough to be proclaimed a different sub-species by biologists, but there are slight genetic differences.

East coast fish are also distinguished from those on the west side by their environment. Deep water runs close to shore on this coast and the Florida current always provides a warm-water refuge. That means they avoid the winter stress experienced by west coast fish on the broad flats. And, the icy fronts that hit in winter blow in

Snook on Florida's east coast grow faster and attain larger average sizes than those on the west coast. The abundance of food and year-around warm water are probably the keys.

from the northwest. Their effect is much stronger on the west coast than on the east, where the waters are protected by Florida's land mass.

Another advantage for Atlantic fish; enormous schools of mullet pass in fall and winter to provide a tremendous bonus food supply in addition to the usual spread of sardines, menhaden, balao and mojarra. And since the mullet are most common in winter, there are no real hard times, as experienced by many fish that must crowd into Gulf Coast rivers where bait is scarce in winter. Whatever the reason, the snook grow faster and reach larger sizes on the east coast.

According to state biologists, a three-year-old west coast female snook is just under 22 inches long, while a three-year-old east coast female tapes over 26 inches. At age five, the west coast fish is around 26.5 inches long, while the east coast female has reached more than 30 inches.

What's more, the fish tend to be much stouter on the east coast. Captain Mike Holiday of Stuart, a writer for Florida Sportsman Magazine, took a 44-inch fish in St. Lucy Inlet that went over 40 pounds on his hand scales. The snook appeared to be much deeper and fatter than typical west coast fish based on a photo he showed me; he had no girth measurement.

As a point of comparison, I saw a 42-incher weighed in at Port of the Islands a few years ago, and that fish went only 26 pounds. A 39-incher I caught there weighed just 18 pounds. And a fishing friend of mine who prefers to be known simply as "Richard the Snooker" caught a 49 1/2" long monster at one of the passes between St. Pete Beach and Dunedin (he'll kill me if I tell which one) that went 42 pounds. That same fish with east coast breadth would have been pushing 50 pounds.

The most successful anglers on the east coast use the same techniques as west coasters, fishing live scaled sardines or greenbacks over areas where the snook school.

In summer, countless millions of these baitfish move into the surf to spawn. In fact, there are so many that on a calm morning they scent the air with a heavy, fishy scent that is reminiscent of cod liver oil. As far as you can see up the beach the fish are flipping and pelicans are diving on them, and every now and then there's the explosion of a snook hitting.

INLET ACTION

Fishing is best in the inlets, including Canaveral, Sebastian, Ft. Pierce, St. Lucie, Jupiter, Palm Beach, Boca Raton, Hillsboro, Lauderdale, Haulover and Government Cut at Miami. The water in these passes tends to be air-clear when winds are calm, as they often are in summer, and you can easily see the pods of fish, usually stacked up at channel edges or around rocky outcroppings.

The technique is simple. The fish wait facing into the tide for finger mullet to be swept out of the passes, and anglers use lures about the size, shape and color of the baitfish. The glittering bits of plastic are allowed to sink deep, ticking just off bottom in 6 to 15 feet of water.

As the boat drifts along about 100 feet off the shoreline, anglers cast slightly to the rear of the boat and allow the tide to bring the lure skimming along, tapping bottom occasionally. When a fish grabs the lure, it stops abruptly, and the momentum of the boat usually sets the hook.

The technique continues to work well throughout the summer, with lots of fish remaining in the passes until the fall mullet run begins sometime between mid-September and mid-October. At that time they pull out and move along the beaches to feed on the traveling schools, an equally productive fishery but one which demands different techniques.

Live baits are also deadly in the inlets, of course, and some of the largest catches are made by anglers who net live menhaden or sardines and use them to chum the fish into a frenzy before tossing their hooked baits in front of them.

"There are times when a little of everything comes in the inlet," says Mark Nichols, a Stuart lure-maker and angling expert.

"You might get a snook on one cast, a king mackerel on the next, then a bonito and finally maybe jump a tarpon. It keeps things interesting."

Small boats work well along the entire eastern shore so long as the wind is from the west, but the waters in the passes here quickly become very dangerous in an easterly breeze, particularly when an outgoing tide causes the waves to "stand up" taller than normal. Locals recommend fishing by boat in the area only for fishermen used to dealing with strong tides and occasional unexpected waves, and when the east wind blows, everybody stays well clear of the passes and beaches.

BEACHES AND BRIDGES

Fish also move along the beaches, congregating in areas where there are inshore reefs or rocks. The House of Refuge rocks at Stuart are a prime example. At Cape Canaveral, there are some real logs in the sub basin, where water depths exceed 60 feet.

On high tides, the snook sometimes move within surfcasting distance of the jetties and beach rocks. Some record-sized fish have been caught by wading anglers in recent years. However, it's better to have a boat in case you have to look for the fish—or in case you have to chase a big one.

Snooking on the east coast is also very dependable around the dozens of bridges that span the Intra-coastal Waterway. The ones that are nearest the inlets and with the deepest flow underneath are

136

During the October mullet run, many big snook as well as tarpon are caught from rocky areas along the Atlantic beaches from Canaveral southward.

usually best, but any bridge over brackish water is worth trying. In fact, the snook sometime prowl for miles up the residential canals here, feeding among the trash tossed out by civilization.

Anywhere there's a dam with flowing water, there will be snook on the saltwater side, as well. There are fewer rivers on the east coast than on the west in snook country, but the Miami River, Lake Worth Creek, the St. Lucie and the Loxahatchee rivers are all worth trying, particularly in winter.

Most anglers chase the fish in small boats, including flats rigs, which are adequate for fishing the passes and the beach on calm mornings. They chum the fish with "free" sardines, then put out the baited hooks and hang on.

ARTIFICIALS ON THE EAST COAST

The usual snook jigs and plugs become more effective as you move into the darker water coming out of the rivers and the green water of the passes. They also work well after dark. In fact, a favorite tactic for bridge fishermen is to "bridge troll" after sundown by walking a 1/2 ounce bucktail trimmed with porkrind or a sinking plug like the 65 M along the pilings. Trolling large diving plugs including the 102 M around the bridges after dark also is effective.

There are some casting opportunities around the residential docks found along most of the Intracoastal. Particularly in areas where the water has a bit of color and where there are grassy shallows right up to the dock line, you can pull fish to 10 pounds out from under the structures on topwaters and on soft plastic jerkbaits. And there are a few bombers of 20 pounds and more cruising the deeper boat channels that are dredged into many of these areas.

Best results come from wading—the fish often spot a boat a long way off. A bonus of this type of fishing is that you occasionally hook up with a jumbo trout—don't forget, the Indian River strain of trout also grow faster and get larger than the west coast trout, and with the netban and tight recreational regulations in place, those big yellowmouths should come back, too.

A very detailed book, including maps with marked snook spots and all boat ramps in Martin & St. Lucie counties is available from Smillie and Associates, 1837 SE Federal Hwy., Stuart, FL 34994. The 75-page "Fisherman's Guide" by Robin Smillie of Florida Sportsman Magazine covers all the bases right down to the best approach for each spot. It's $11.95 including postage.

CHAPTER 16

MASTERING THE EVERGLADES

The southern tip of Florida is one of the few parts of the state that still remains much as it was when the Seminoles ruled, a sprawl of land only inches above the sea, endless jungle rivers and creeks, mangroves and sawgrass marshes, a vast, wondrous mixing of fresh water with salt where snook and many other species thrive, and where man is still a visitor and not a resident.

The entire stretch from Marco Island to Key Largo looks as if there should be a snook under every mangrove limb. That's the problem with fishing here. It all looks good, but like anywhere else in snook country, the fish concentrate in only a few spots, and those spots change with the seasons.

According to the calendar, the snook in the 10,000 Islands are supposed to be sunbathing along the beaches by the full moon in May, spawning in the passes by night. But the fish pay closer attention to water temperature than to the calendar. A few years ago on an usually cold spring, I visited over Memorial Day weekend.

Fishing out of Port of the Islands Resort east of Naples, I was encouraged to see a fleet of flats boats, perhaps a dozen in all, lined up at the floating docks.

And when first light came, we all dutifully proceeded down the canal (a 40-minute putt at idle speed due to the four-mile-long manatee zone) headed for the outer islands and passes where the fish were "supposed" to be.

Areas where the fresh waters of the Everglades join the salty water of the 10,000 Islands can be great snooking spots, particularly when heavy rains increase the flow. Snook readily attack freshwater prey including bluegills and shiners.

And we all flailed said wild and seemingly endless water to a froth—and came up with goose-eggs. Even some of my favored honey holes, developed over 20 years of fishing out of the Port, turned up empty.

Where did the snook go?

Nowhere, actually. They were still where they had been all winter.

UP THE CREEK

On the last day, because time was short and rain clouds threatened, I didn't go all the way to the mouth of the Fakka Union River, but instead cut off into the back country, traveling back north and west after leaving the marked channel.

And there, in a deep creek where the splash of leaping mullet beckoned, we found fish.

They were knocking finger mullet up into the mangrove roots. They were pushing big vee wakes in the flat, black water. They were "finning" in the shallows, loafing along on top, their yellow fins and tails breaking the surface.

140

From that point on the only trick was to find an artificial that looked somewhat like the finger mullet. The fish readily hit topwater plugs. Most were typical 20- to 25-inch fish, and they threw themselves on the plugs with explosive hits that had us tossing backlashes and hooking each other as often as the fish in a wild, hour-long melee.

Just before it ended, I spotted a cruiser pushing water about 100 feet out. I pitched a floater 20 feet ahead of the wake, began working it fast, and was rewarded as the fish charged, blew up on the lure and knocked it three feet into the air. When the bait landed, it struck again, and missed again.

The fish then chased the plug to within 20 feet of the boat before sinking out of sight. I reeled in, talking to myself, but still able to make a quick but bad cast to the area where the giant had disappeared—and up she came immediately to catch the lure sideways.

The fish made a long run down the creek, ending with a ponderous headshake that brought only head and shoulders out of the water; she was too big to jump clear. In about 10 minutes, the baitcasting rig finished the job and I lipped the fish, a 38-inch trophy.

A few photos and we slipped her back into the murky water, none the worse for the wear. The same couldn't be said of my lure, which had the tail hook bent into a pretzel from the force of her jaws.

FEAST OR FAMINE

The 10,000 Islands area has a way of treating anglers to either feast or famine. The fish are often tightly bunched in only a few miles of all those millions of acres of estuary. Find the magic zone where the temperature, salinity, water clarity and available baitfish are just right, and you find the motherlode. Miss it and the area is a very so-so fishery.

Don Causey, who publishes the "Angling Report" newsletter in Miami, is one fisherman who has learned the vagaries of the area.

"If I can't find fish, I head inland, especially in late fall, winter and early spring," says Causey. "If you go up where there are spider webs across the creeks, you're fishing the frontier, and a lot of times that's where the fish are."

Causey mostly fishes topwaters, and reports some 50-snook days by heading into the backcountry out of Flamingo or Chokoloskee. But he also reports getting skunked now and then.

Feast or famine, it's the name of the game.

CHART YOUR COURSE

The trick to find fish here is first to get your hands on a chart. You simply can't begin to find your way through the thousands of unmarked channels and unnamed islands without a chart in hand— you'll get lost almost immediately, and you're also highly likely to go aground in areas where the shallow water extends for miles.

You can't do better than the Florida Sportsman Fishing Chart series, which go for $6.95 each. They're printed on waterproof paper and have many fishing hotspots marked. To fish the 10,000 Islands area you need Number 705, while the eastern Everglades is covered by Number 704. They're available from Florida Sportsman, 5901 S.W. 74th St, Miami, FL 33143, tel. (305) 661-4222.

It's also not a bad idea to carry a GPS. One of the portable charting systems like the Lowrance Global Map Sport is handy for a flats rig because it stays in the console until you get lost. And these units show all the un-named islands and channels, plus your exact position among them.

Of course, they don't show much in the way of depth, so you still have to punch your way in and out, but at least you won't have to spend the night with the 'skeeters. (The mosquitoes and no-see-ums are fierce throughout the area, of course. Take Avon Skin-So-Soft or Johnson Skintastic for the no-see-ums, lots of high-DEET repellant like Deep Woods Off for the mosquitoes. If you fish still, summer nights, you'll need long sleeves, long pants and a headnet, too. A Shoo-Bug net suit is also effective, and you can slather it with Permanone or 100 percent DEET that you shouldn't put on bare skin.)

Interestingly, the fish migrations throughout the area tend to be north and south, so when you find snook three miles up one river, you're likely to find fish three miles up several others nearby.

HOT SPOTS

Some of my personal favorite areas out of Port of the Islands include the S's of the Fakka Union on a falling tide, the mouth of

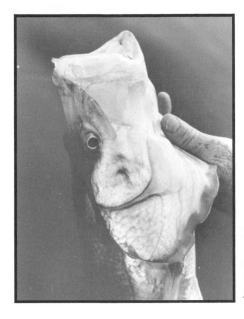

The difficult navigation in the 'Glades helps preserve large snook. For those who learn the water, the muddy creeks can provide outstanding action.

the East River, also on the fall, the shores of Fakahatchee Bay on the rise, and the shoals around Panther Key and Tiger Key.

All of this is fairly civilized fishing because if you get lost going west you can always work out to the Gulf and see the highrises of Marco Island about 15 miles off in the distance. If you get lost going east, you're likely to cut the Indian Key Pass markers which lead to Everglades City.

Proceed much farther east, though, and you enter no-man's land—but also perhaps the best fishing, since fewer anglers make the run into remote areas like the Huston River, Chatham River, the appropriately-named Lostman's River, Shark River and those beyond stretching toward Flamingo.

All of these rivers harbor snook, which gather around island points and deep mangrove shores on high water and creek mouths on the fall. They also have good numbers of tarpon from 2 to 60 pounds, most often found in the deeper, open stretches. And you'll hook reds and snapper along the shores as well, particularly if you tip a jig with a bit of shrimp.

Everglades snook migrate north and south rather than east and west like most west coast snook. They're usually found on the outside beaches and passes in May and June, but may be miles up the dark creeks in December.

The harbor at Port of the Islands is itself a noted snook hotspot. The area is dredged to eight feet and thus provides a temperature refuge year-around. And the Fakka Union River drops over a low dam here, aerating the water and frequently pushing freshwater shiners and bream down to waiting snook below. The fresh water also attracts mullet year around, which in turn attract snook, tarpon and jacks.

(The resort, incidentally, is the only Florida location mentioned in A.J. McClane's book, "Great Fishing Resorts of the World." The book was written more than a decade ago, but the Port still stands as one of the most angler-friendly spots in the state. It has all the goodies, marina, ramp, floating docks, and a good restaurant where you can get coffee early and dinner late. The lengthy manatee zone is bothersome, but often you don't even have to leave the channel to find outstanding fishing. Phone there is (941) 394-3101).

While you're in the area, treat yourself to a dinner at the old Everglades Rod & Gun Club. This ancient structure is a Florida classic. It stands on the shores of the Barron River, and can be reached by boat via the marked channel or by car by following U.S.

Snook proceed to the outside islands and cuts between May and the end of September each year. Larry Larsen found some spectacular fishing in the deep channels that flow between the islands and flats on the days approaching new and full moons.

41 and State Route 29. The food is super, though a bit pricey, and the atmosphere is right out of the 1920's. (No air-conditioning, but the ceiling fans keep you cool except in the dead of summer —and take cash. They don't accept credit cards.)

FISHING THE OUTSIDE

The snook do proceed to the outside islands and cuts, eventually, sometime between May and the end of September each year. You can experience some spectacular fishing in the deep channels that flow between the islands and flats on the days approaching new and full moons right through September. The fish usually hang in spawning aggregations when they're on the outside, and where you catch one you may catch 10.

The classic tactic is to drift the deepest cuts—up to 12 foot depths—on outgoing tide with live pinfish, grunts or sardines floated along a foot or so off bottom. A 65M ticked along bottom also works well.

But you can also find action by poling the edges and making long casts with topwater plugs, particularly early and late in the day and after dark. Wading along the beaches is also a good approach, and less likely to spook fish. High or rising water seems best for this. You need a good breeze to keep the bugs away, though. And watch for small stingrays. In spring, there are hundreds of them.

Inside or outside, the 'Glades are classic snook country where every serious snooker should pay homage at least once. The fish are big and wild, and you can sometimes fish for hours without sight of another boat. This is what snook fishing was meant to be.

Unfortunately, there's a murky cloud over the Glades. Poor water quality coming down from the farmlands around Okeechobee appear to have caused a huge "dead zone" in Florida Bay, where thousands of acres of sea grasses have died. This sort of habitat destruction is sure to have an impact on gamefish numbers, and it's a cancer that has to be removed. Government efforts to clean up the outflows are underway, but it's going to be a long struggle and one that will require the support of all anglers to come to a good end.

CHAPTER 17

MASTER GUIDES & TIPS

There are no shortcuts to becoming a snook master. It takes time and effort and persistence. But fishing with a guide definitely shortens the learning curve.

Guides spend 200 days per year or more on the water. They know where the fish are day after day, tide after tide, in every season of the year.

The recreational angler takes many years to accumulate that sort of experience. Many give up before they ever attain enough success to really begin to enjoy snook fishing. Yet, a few days with a guide—for about the price of a couple of boat payments—could bring a quantum leap in their skill levels.

The following list is far from exhaustive, but it does include a lot of true snook-masters who have taught me much. One caution; many are booked weeks or months in advance. Call early.

Fred Arledge, Tampa Bay, (813) 949-5451
Raymond Baird, Jupiter (407) 746-5266
Mark Bennett, Tarpon Springs-Hudson (813) 848-8747
Larry Blue, Clearwater, (813) 595-4798
Brad Bradley, Weeki Wachee (904) 596-5639
John Carlisle, Everglades (941) 695-2244
Phil Chapman, Charlotte Harbor (941) 646-9445
Tom Chaya, Sarasota Bay, (941) 778-4498
Butch Constable, Jupiter (407) 747-6665
Dave Eimers, Marco (941) 353-4828
Eric Ersch, Canaveral (407) 779-9054
Greg Gentile, Port St. Lucie (407) 878-0475
Pete Greenan, Charlotte Harbor (941) 923-6095

John Griffith, Tampa Bay (813) 238-5910
Rick Gross, Sarasota Bay, (941) 794-3308
Paul Hawkins, Tampa Bay (813) 526-2438
Steve Hayes, Stuart/Vero (407) 778-9654
Steve Hogan, Charlotte Harbor (941) 474-6461
Van Hubbard, Charlotte Harbor (941) 697-6944
Richard Knox, Tarpon Springs (813) 376-8809
Ron Kowalyk, Estero Bay, (941) 267-9312
John Kumiski, Everglades, (407) 834-2954
Larry Lazoen, Port Charlotte (941) 627-1704
Dave Markett, Tarpon Springs/Tampa Bay (813) 962-1435
Rob McCue, Tarpon Springs (813) 843-0489
Tim McOsker, Charlotte Harbor, (941) 475-5908
Sandy Melvin, Charlotte Harbor, (800) 962-3314
Chris Mitchell, Charlotte Harbor (941) 964-2887
Scott Moore, Charlotte Harbor/Tampa Bay (941) 778-3005
Brian Mowatt, Charlotte Harbor (941) 624-4920
Jim O'Neal, Tampa Bay (941) 794-5960
Dave Pomerleau, Tampa Bay (813) 577-8076
Dan Prickett, Chokoloskee (941) 695-4573
John Royall, Indian River (407) 452-0863
Dennis Royston, New Port Richey (813) 863-3204
Bob Sabatino, Pine Island Sound (941) 752-1451
Eric Shapiro, Tampa Bay (813) 963-1930
Russ Sirmons, St. Petersburg (813) 526-2090
Mike Talkington, Southern Tampa Bay (813) 754-3738
Tom Tamanini, Tampa Bay (813) 581-4942
Ray Van Horn, Tarpon Springs (813) 938-8577
Pete Villani, Naples, (941) 262-8228, 455-2334
Johnnie Walker, Sarasota Bay, (941) 922-2287
Jerry Williams, Tampa Bay (813) 254-5289
James Wisner, Tampa Bay (813) 831-5659
James Wood, Terra Ceia (941) 722-8746

TIPS FROM SNOOK MASTERS

The following bag of tricks contains gems that may turn a poor trip into a good one.

CLEAR WATER

When you can see snook, they can see you, says snook master Bob Sabatino of Captiva. Crystal clear water is the enemy of the snooker. The fish bite better in water with a pale green shade, or in tannin-stained water of the backcountry where the visibility is not so clear.

Birds don't waste energy diving for fun. Where there are pelicans, herons and egrets, there's snook food. Be alert for such clues when you search for fish.

If you have to fish them in clear water, choose live bait rather than lures, make long casts, wade and use light tackle. Six-pound-test line and 20-pound-test leader draws a lot more strikes in high-vis water than does 15-pound-test with 40-pound shock.

FIND MULLET, FIND SNOOK

Like trout and redfish, snook tend to travel with mullet schools. They often swim with mullet that are over 5 pounds, much too big for them to eat. Why do they do it? Maybe it's a defense strategy against porpoises, which love to eat snook. Possibly traveling with the more numerous mullet give the snook a disguise, as well as offering the porpoise easier targets.

In any case, big snook and mullet go together on both coasts. Watch for the area where the mullet travel along a shore and you'll see snook cruising there at some point during the tide cycle. You can find the mullet by watching for them to jump. And along many shorelines, mullet have a sort of path that they follow at given tide cycles—the "mullet line", Capt. Russ Sirmons calls it. Learn where they travel and you can sit there and wait for the mullet to draw snook to you.

LUNKER LIGHTS

Around lights, you may see only small snook on top, but many times, particularly in passes and over deep water, there are lunkers down below. Sink the bait, or use one that's too big for the juniors and you may connect with a whopper.

Lots of scouting is required to locate spots that produce doubles of this size. There's no substitute for hours on the water —fish as often as you can. (MirrOlure photo)

Around lights that are easily fished—those with catwalks or docks adjacent—bigger fish are likely to be scarce. But find one that can't be accessed except by boat and you may have a hotspot.

WINDAGE

Pay attention to the wind, as well. If it's strong, it will affect your cast. Make allowance so that your first shot goes right where it needs to be—the first cast is often the one that produces if everything is right.

Remember that a wind over the shoulder allows longer casts, particularly if you arc them high. A wind in the face shortens a cast unless you sidearm it low.

DOCK SNOOK

Captain Dave Pomerleau notes that large snook are often scavengers, so it's wise to check out cleaning tables around docks, particularly after dark when things get quiet. The steady stream of carcasses create an easy feeding area for big, lazy fish.

He says that the biggest fish have scars on their bellies and often have the tips of anal fins and tails worn off, evidence, he thinks, that they lie on bottom all day, often cleaning up leftovers, rising up only after dark to feed on live food.

Larsen's Outdoor Publishing
OUTDOORS/NATURE
RESOURCE DIRECTORY

If you are interested in more productive fishing, hunting and diving trips, this information is for you!

Learn how to be more successful on your next outdoor venture from these secrets, tips and tactics. Larsen's Outdoor Publishing offers informational-type books that focus on how and where to catch the most popular sport fish, hunt the most popular game or travel to productive or exciting destinations.

The perfect-bound, soft-cover books include numerous illustrative graphics, line drawings, maps and photographs. Many of our **LIBRARIES** are nationwide in scope. Others cover the Gulf and Atlantic coasts from Florida to Texas to Maryland and some foreign waters. One **SERIES** focuses on the top lakes, rivers and creeks in the nation's most visited largemouth bass fishing state.

> ### THANKS!
> *"I appreciate the research you've done to enhance the sport for weekend anglers." R. Willis,*

All series appeal to outdoors readers of all skill levels. The unique four-color cover design, interior layout, quality, information content and economical price makes these books your best source of knowledge. **Best of all, you will know how to be more successful in your outdoor endeavors!!**

SALTWATER ENTHUSIASTS!

Check out the Inshore Library & the Secret Spots books -- guaranteed to help you catch more of your favorite saltwater species!
Take a look at the Fish & Dive Series for a new perspective on these popular sports!

See the following pages for more information and the discount order form!

BASS SERIES LIBRARY
by Larry Larsen

(BSL1) FOLLOW THE FORAGE - BASS/PREY RELATIONSHIP - Learn how to determine dominant forage in a body of water and catch more bass!

(BSL2) BETTER BASS ANGLING TECHNIQUES - Learn why one lure or bait is more successful than others and how to use each lure under varying conditions.

(BSL3) BASS PRO STRATEGIES - Professional fishermen know how changes in pH, water level, temperature and color affect bass fishing, and they know how to adapt to weather and topographical variations. Learn from their experience.

(BSL4) BASS LURES - TRICKS & TECHNIQUES - Bass become accustomed to the same artificials and presentations seen over and over again and become harder to catch. Modify your lures and rigs and develop new presentation and retrieve methods to spark the interest of largemouth!

(BSL5) SHALLOW WATER BASS - Bass spend 90% of their time in waters less than 15 feet deep. Apply these productive new tactics and triple your results!

(BSL6) BASS FISHING FACTS - Learn why and how bass behave during pre- and post-spawn, how they utilize their senses when active and how they respond to their environment, and you'll increase your bass angling success!

(BSL7) TROPHY BASS - If you're more interested in wrestling with one or two monster largemouth than with a "panful" of yearlings, then learn what techniques and locations will improve your chances.

(BSL8) ANGLER'S GUIDE TO BASS PATTERNS - Catch bass every time out by learning how to develop a productive pattern quickly and effectively. "Bass Patterns" is a reference source for all anglers, regardless of where they live or their skill level. Learn how to choose the right lure, presentation and habitat under various weather and environmental conditions!

(BSL9) BASS GUIDE TIPS - Learn secret techniques known only in a certain region or state that often work in waters all around the country. It's this new approach that usually results in excellent bass angling success. Learn how to apply what the country's top guides know!

Nine Great Volumes To Help You Catch More and Larger Bass!

(LB1) LARRY LARSEN ON BASS TACTICS

is the ultimate "how-to" book that focuses on proven productive methods. Hundreds of highlighted tips and drawings in our LARSEN ON BASS SERIES explain how you can catch more and larger bass in waters all around the country. This reference source by America's best known bass fishing writer will be invaluable to both the avid novice and expert angler!

(PF1) PEACOCK BASS EXPLOSIONS! by Larry Larsen

A must read for those anglers who are interested in catching the world's most exciting fresh water fish! Detailed tips, trip planning and tactics for peacocks in South Florida, Venezuela, Brazil, Puerto Rico, Hawaii and other destinations. This book explores the most effective tactics to take the aggressive peacock bass. Invaluable to all adventurous anglers!

(PF2) PEACOCK BASS & OTHER FIERCE EXOTICS by Larry Larsen

Book 2 in the Series reveals the latest techniques and best spots to prepare you for the greatest fishing experience of your life! You'll learn how to catch more and larger fish using the valuable information from the author and expert angler, a four-time peacock bass world-record holder. It's the first comprehensive discussion on this wild and colorful fish. With stops in Peru, Colombia, Venezuela and Brazil, he provides information about colorful monster payara, and other exotic fish.

BASS WATERS GUIDE SERIES by Larry Larsen

The most productive bass waters are described in this multi-volume series, including ramps, seasonal tactics, water characteristics, etc. Many maps and photos detail specific locations.

(BW1) GUIDE TO NORTH FLORIDA BASS WATERS - Covers from Orange Lake north and west. Includes Lakes Lochloosa, Talquin and Seminole, the St. Johns, Nassau, Suwannee and Apalachicola Rivers; Newnans Lake, St. Mary's River, Juniper Lake, Ortega River, Lake Jackson, Deer Point Lake, Panhandle Mill Ponds and many more!

(BW2) GUIDE TO CENTRAL FLORIDA BASS WATERS - From Tampa/Orlando to Palatka. Includes Lakes George, Rodman, Monroe, Tarpon, the Harris Chain, the St.

Johns, Oklawaha, Withlacoochee, Crystal and Hillsborough Rivers, Conway Chain, Homosassa River, Lake Minneola, Lake Weir, Spring Runs and more!

(BW3) GUIDE TO SOUTH FLORIDA BASS WATERS - From I-4 to the Everglades. Includes Lakes Toho, Kissimmee, Okeechobee, Poinsett, Tenoroc and Blue Cypress, the Winter Haven Chain, Caloosahatchee River, the Everglades, and more!

OUTDOOR TRAVEL SERIES
by Larry Larsen and M. Timothy O'Keefe

Candid guides on the best charters, time of the year, and other recommendations that can make your next fishing and/or diving trip much more enjoyable.

(OT1) FISH & DIVE THE CARIBBEAN Vol. 1
Northern Caribbean, including Cozumel, Cayman Islands, Bahamas, Jamaica, Virgin Islands. Required reading for fishing and diving enthusiasts who want to know the most cost-effective means to enjoy these and other Caribbean islands.

> **BEST BOOK CONTENT!**
> *"Fish & Dive the Caribbean" was a finalist in the Best Book Content Category of the National Association of Independent Publishers (NAIP). Over 500 books were submitted by publishers including Simon & Schuster and Turner Publishing. Said the judges "An excellent source book with invaluable instructions. Written by two nationally-known experts who, indeed, know what vacationing can be!"*

(OT3) FISH & DIVE FLORIDA & The Keys - Where and how to plan a vacation to America's most popular fishing and diving destination. Features include artificial reef loran numbers; freshwater springs/caves; coral reefs/barrier islands; gulf stream/passes; inshore flats/channels; and back country estuaries.

DIVING / NATURE SERIES by M. Timothy O'Keefe

(DL2) MANATEES - OUR VANISHING MERMAIDS is an in-depth overview of nature's strangest-looking, gentlest animals. They're among America's most endangered mammals. The book covers where to see manatees while diving, why they may be living fossils, their unique life cycle, and much more.

(DL3) SEA TURTLES - THE WATCHERS' GUIDE - Discover how and where you can witness sea turtles nesting in Florida. This book not only gives an excellent overview of sea turtle life, it also provides the specifics of appropriate personal conduct and behavior for human beings on turtle nesting beaches.

OUTDOOR ADVENTURE by Vin T. Sparano, Outdoor Life

(OA1) HUNTING DANGEROUS GAME - Live the adventure of hunting those dangerous animals that hunt back! Track a rogue elephant, survive a grizzly attack. These classic tales will make you very nervous next time you're in the woods!

> **KEEP ME UPDATED!**
> *"I would like to get on your mailing list. I really enjoy your books!"*
> G. Granger, Cypress, CA

(OA2) GAME BIRDS & GUN DOGS - A unique collection of tales about hunters, their dogs and the upland game and waterfowl they hunt. You will read about good gun dogs and heart-breaking dogs, but never about bad dogs, because there's no such animal.

COASTAL FISHING GUIDES
by Frank Sargeant

A unique "where-to" series of detailed secret spots for Florida's finest saltwater fishing. These guide books describe hundreds of little-known honeyholes and exactly how to fish them. Prime seasons, baits and lures, marinas and dozens of detailed maps of the prime spots are included. The comprehensive index helps the reader to further pinpoint productive areas and tactics. Over $160 worth of personally-marked NOAA charts in the two books.

(FG1) SECRET SPOTS Tampa Bay to Cedar Key
Covers Hillsborough River and Davis Island through the Manatee River, Mullet Key and the Suwannee River.

(FG2) SECRET SPOTS Southwest Florida
Covers from Sarasota Bay to Marco.

INSHORE SERIES by Frank Sargeant

(IL1) THE SNOOK BOOK-Every aspect of how you can find and catch big snook is covered, in all seasons and all waters where snook are found.

(IL2) THE REDFISH BOOK-Packed with every aspect of finding and fooling giant reds. You'll learn secret techniques revealed for the first time. After reading this informative book, you'll catch more redfish on your next trip!

(IL3) THE TARPON BOOK-Find and catch the wily "silver king" along the Gulf Coast, north through the mid-Atlantic, and south along Central and South American coastlines.

(IL4) THE TROUT BOOK -Jammed with tips for both the old salt and the rank amateur who pursue the spotted weakfish, or seatrout, throughout the coastal waters of the Gulf and Atlantic.

SEND ME MORE!
"I am delighted with Frank Sargeant's Redfish Book. Please let me know when others in the Inshore Series will be available."
J.A'Hern, Columbia, S.C.

GIFT ORDER!
"I have three of your Inshore Series books. My daughter just moved to Homosassa and I want to send her the same books!."
N. Pappas, Bonita Springs, FL

SALTWATER SERIES by Frank Sargeant

(SW1) THE REEF FISHING BOOK - A compilation of the best techniques, lures and locations for grouper and snapper and other reef species, including how to find and catch live bait, trolling techniques and the latest rod and reels. Learn the secrets of top charterboat professionals for finding and catching big grouper and snapper throughout their 2,000-mile coastal range. Special features include where the biggest fish live, electronics savvy, anchoring tricks and more!

(SW2) THE MASTERS BOOK OF SNOOK - Learn the secrets of top professional skippers for finding and catching giant snook from Florida to South America. The latest tactics include lots of biological data never before printed in the public press. The ultimate snook book for the ultimate snook fisherman.

LARSEN'S OUTDOOR PUBLISHING
CONVENIENT ORDER FORM
ALL PRICES INCLUDE POSTAGE/HANDLING

FRESH WATER
___ BSL1. Better Bass Angling Vol 1 ($13.95)
___ BSL2. Better Bass Angling Vol 2 ($13.95)
___ BSL3. Bass Pro Strategies ($13.95)
___ BSL4. Bass Lures/Techniques ($13.95)
___ BSL5. Shallow Water Bass ($13.95)
___ BSL6. Bass Fishing Facts ($13.95)
___ BSL7. Trophy Bass ($13.95)
___ BSL8. Bass Patterns ($13.95)
___ BSL9. Bass Guide Tips ($13.95)
___ CF1. Mstrs' Scrts/Crappie Fshng ($12.45)
___ CF2. Crappie Tactics ($12.45)
___ CF3. Mstr's Secrets of Catfishing ($12.45)
___ LB1. Larsen on Bass Tactics ($15.45)
___ PF1. Peacock Bass Explosions! ($16.95)
___ PF2. Peacock Bass & Other Fierce
        Exotics ($17.95)

SALT WATER
___ IL1. The Snook Book   ($13.95)
___ IL2. The Redfish Book ($13.95)
___ IL3. The Tarpon Book ($13.95)
___ IL4. The Trout Book ($13.95)
___ SW1. The Reef Fishing Book ($16.45)
___ SW2. The Masters Book of Snook ($16.45)

OTHER OUTDOORS BOOKS
___ DL2. Manatees/Vanishing ($11.45)
___ DL3. Sea Turtles/Watchers' ($11.45)

REGIONAL
___ FG1. Secret Spots-Tampa Bay/
           Cedar Key ($15.45)
___ FG2. Secret Spots - SW Florida ($15.45)
___ BW1. Guide/North Fl. Waters ($14.95)
___ BW2. Guide/Cntral Fl.Waters ($14.95)
___ BW3. Guide/South Fl.Waters ($14.95)
___ OT1. Fish/Dive - Caribbean   ($11.95)
___ OT3. Fish/Dive Florida/ Keys ($13.95)

HUNTING
___ DH1. Mstrs' Secrets/ Deer Hunting ($13.95)
___ DH2. Science of Deer Hunting ($13.95)
___ DH3. Mstrs' Secrets/Bowhunting ($12.45)
___ DH4. How to Take Monster Bucks ($13.95)
___ TH1. Mstrs' Secrets/ Turkey Hunting ($13.95)
___ OA1. Hunting Dangerous Game! ($9.95)
___ OA2. Game Birds & Gun Dogs ($9.95)

BOOKS & DISCOUNT PACKAGES

___ BSL - Bass Series Library (9 vol. set) $94.45
___ IL -   Inshore Library (4 vol. set) $42.95
___ BW - Guides to Bass Waters (3 vols.) $37.95

Volume sets are autographed by each author.

BIG MULTI-BOOK DISCOUNT!
2-3 books, SAVE 10%
4 or more books, SAVE 20%

INTERNATIONAL ORDERS
Send check in U.S. funds; add $6
more per book for airmail rate

ALL PRICES INCLUDE POSTAGE/HANDLING

No. of books _____ *x $* _____ *ea =$* _____ | *Special Package* _____ *@ $* _____
No. of books _____ *x $* _____ *ea =$* _____ | *(Pkgs include discount)= N/A*
Multi-book Discount (_____ *%) $* _____
      SUBTOTAL 1   *$* _____ | *SUBTOTAL 2*   *$* _____

_____ **For Priority Mail (add $2 more per book)** $_____
TOTAL ENCLOSED (check or money order) $_____

NAME _____ *ADDRESS* _____

CITY _____ *STATE* _____ *ZIP* _____

Send check or Money Order to: Larsen's Outdoor Publishing, Dept. SW2
2640 Elizabeth Place, Lakeland, FL 33813 (941)644-3381
(Sorry, no credit card orders)

INDEX